"*The Gospel-Centered Life for Teens* is a remarkable, easy-to-use curriculum for helping young adults go deeper into the glories of all that God has done for us in Christ. Important theological concepts—including God's holiness, our sinfulness, and the relationship between the law and the gospel—are explained in simple, clear, and compelling language. This is a resource that can simultaneously introduce teens to Christ and help committed Christians grow in their faith. I'm excited to recommend it."
    Alex Chediak, Professor at California Baptist University; author of *Thriving at College: Make Great Friends, Keep Your Faith, and Get Ready for the Real World!*

"Fantastic study! Creative, innovative, refreshing, and biblically focused!"
    Joe White, President of Kanakuk Kamps

"I know so many teens who need these lessons. They're living in an image-gripped world where acceptance seems based on this or that label. *The Gospel-Centered Life for Teens* turns that on its head, steadily and sweetly pointing students to 'the only label that really matters: "in Christ."'
    What great lessons! They take on the tough issues teens deal with every day, like gossip and greed, and they show how believing the gospel changes everything. I wish every teen I know could do this study."
    Jack Klumpenhower, Author of *Show Them Jesus: Teaching the Gospel to Kids*

"Thune and Walker have given us a gift by reminding us that we never move past our need for the gospel. It is always shaping, always informing, and always transforming us more and more into the image of Christ. If you want a clear, easy-to-understand guide for teens on the theology and application of the gospel in your life, this guide is for you!"
    Brian Cosby, Author of *Giving Up Gimmicks: Reclaiming Youth Ministry from an Entertainment Culture*

"The gospel is a crucial topic for this next generation and one we must invest in as we raise up future leaders of the Church. *The Gospel-Centered Life for Teens* is therefore a great and timely resource for helping to form spiritually mature teens with a life cemented in the gospel, which unleashes them to make a profound difference for the Kingdom."
    Dave Ramseyer, Vice President, National Ministries, Youth for Christ (yfc.org)

"All human beings are religious. Everyone worships someone or something. There is always a center to our lives. In a world offering teens a constant barrage of 'centers' that lie and can never fulfill, *The Gospel-Centered Life for Teens* takes them on a much-needed journey into the place where they can hear God's voice, understand God's grand story for their lives, and assume the place for which they've been made."
    Dr. Walt Mueller, Author of *Youth Culture 101*; founder/president of Center for Parent/Youth Understanding

"There is nothing more important in discipling students then helping them grasp the power of the gospel for their own lives. *The Gospel-Centered Life for Teens* is a powerful tool and welcome resource! Many thanks to Will Walker and Bob Thune for developing this excellent tool."
    Chuck Klein, Executive Director, The Campus Alliance

"This distillation of gospel truth for teens is a great tool for churches and ministries that are seeking to raise up the next generation of church and culture leaders. I heartily recommend it."
    Rev. Jason Dorsey, Lead Pastor Redeemer Presbyterian Church, Indianapolis

"*The Gospel-Centered Life for Teens* is a thoughtful, age-appropriate adaptation of *The Gospel-Centered Life*. I like using *GCL* for one reason: it helpfully illuminates just how big the gospel really is for people like you and me living out our lives right here and now. It helps people like us see that following Jesus affects more of our lives than we might ever have imagined. It's relentlessly relational and hopeful."
    Aaron Baker, Pastor, Covenant Presbyterian Church of Chicago

"After seeing such great fruit in my years as a youth pastor and small group leader, I'm so thankful that this great curriculum has been rewritten with teens in mind. In twenty-four years of youth ministry and the shepherding of my own four teenage children, I have found no other study so important and foundational in the way they are to think and live as *The Gospel-Centered Life for Teens*. I wholeheartedly recommend it."
    Rev. Mark Kuiper, Senior Pastor Kirk of the Hills Presbyterian Church, St. Louis, MO

THE GOSPEL-CENTERED LIFE FOR TEENS

Robert H. Thune and Will Walker

LEADER'S GUIDE

www.newgrowthpress.com

The Gospel-Centered Life for Teens: Leader's Guide

Copyright © 2014 by Serge.
Published 2014 New Growth Press, Greensboro, NC 27404

All rights reserved. No part of this publication may be reproduced, stored in a retrieval system, or transmitted in any form by any means, electronic, mechanical, photocopy, recording, or otherwise, without the prior permission of the publisher, except as provided by USA copyright law.

Unless otherwise noted, Scripture taken from the HOLY BIBLE, NEW INTERNATIONAL VERSION®. Copyright © 1973, 1978, 1984 by International Bible Society. Used by permission of Zondervan. All rights reserved.

    Additional Scripture quotations are from *The Holy Bible,* English Standard Version, copyright © 2001 by Crossway Bible, a division of Good News Publishers. Used by permission. All rights reserved.

Design: Brett Westervelt
Typesetting & E-book: Lisa Parnell, lparnell.com
Cover Design: Faceout Books, faceoutstudio.com

ISBN: 978-1-939946-70-6 (Print)
ISBN: 978-1-939946-95-9 (eBook)

Printed in the United States of America

21 20 19 18 17 16 15 14   1 2 3 4 5

CONTENTS

INTRODUCTION 1

GOSPEL OVERVIEW 9

Lesson 1- **THE GOSPEL GRID** 13
    Article: *The Gospel Grid*
    Exercise: *Judging Others*

Lesson 2- **PRETENDING** 23
    Article: *Shrinking the Cross: Pretending*
    Exercise: *Six Ways of Minimizing Sin*

Lesson 3- **PERFORMING** 33
    Article: *Shrinking the Cross: Performing*
    Exercise: *Self-Assessment: Orphans vs. Children*

Lesson 4- **LAW & GOSPEL** 45
    Article: *The Law & the Gospel*
    Exercise: *The Gospel Grid & the Law*

Lesson 5- **REPENTANCE** 55
    Article: *Lifestyle Repentance*
    Exercise: *Practicing Repentance*

Lesson 6- **HEART IDOLATRY** 65
    Article: *Heart Idolatry*

Lesson 7–MISSION **73**
    Article: *The Gospel Propels Us Outward*
    Exercise: *Getting to the Heart of Mission*

Lesson 8–FORGIVENESS **83**
    Article: *The Gospel Empowers Us to Forgive*
    Exercise: *Getting to the Heart of Forgiveness*

Lesson 9–CONFLICT **91**
    Article: *The Gospel Helps Us Fight Fairly*
    Exercise: *Gospel-Centered Conflict Resolution*

INTRODUCTION

ABOUT SERGE

Serge never set out to write and publish curriculum. We are a missions agency that has always believed the power and motive for mission is the gospel of grace at work in the life of a believer. However, along the way, we've also discovered that it's a lot harder to do cross-cultural, team-oriented ministry than we thought. Eventually, we started writing material to keep the gospel front and center in our own lives and relationships. Before long we had pastors and ministry leaders requesting gospel-centered materials for use in their churches and ministries.

Over the years, it's been our privilege to partner with friends who share our passion for the way the gospel transforms both believers and unbelievers alike. This study is the result of one such partnership. Bob Thune and Will Walker adapted their study *The Gospel-Centered Life* to make it accessible to teens and help them grow in the gospel. We're partnering with them to publish it because we think it is a helpful and much-needed resource.

Some of the original content was adapted from earlier Serge materials. If you are familiar with *Sonship, Gospel Identity, Gospel Growth,* and *Gospel Love,* you may recognize a few key themes and concepts. If you haven't heard them presented before, Bob and Will have done a great job of articulating the gospel in simple, deep, and transformative ways here.

As a cross-denominational, reformed, sending agency with over 200 missionaries on over 25 teams in 5 continents, Serge is always looking for people who are ready to take the next step in a missional lifestyle. If you'd like to learn more about our teaching, healing, and equipping ministries around the world and what might be next for you, please visit

1

us at www.serge.org/mission. If you'd like to learn more about our gospel mentoring programs and the discipleship training that we offer here in the United States, you can find those details at www.serge.org/mentoring.

FROM THE AUTHORS

God gave us the privilege of planting a wonderfully messy church, where mature Christians, newer Christians, and lots of non-Christians and skeptics are all mixed up together. Our church is structured around these groups called missional communities, which are kind of like traditional church small groups, only completely different.

The ideal missional community consists of a small band of Christians living on mission together, and inviting their non-Christian friends to join in conversation and interaction about the gospel of Jesus. This seemed like a really great idea…until we started doing it. We quickly discovered two significant problems:

> *1. Most traditional "church small group" material was written for a Christian audience, and therefore non-Christians relate to it about as well as a cattle rancher relates to vegetarians.*
>
> *2. Many Christians have a weak and anemic understanding of the gospel, so asking them to talk about how the gospel is transforming them is like asking a teenage boy band to talk about the finer elements of Mozart's work.*

So we wrote The Gospel-Centered Life *in order to shape "gospel DNA" in our church in a way that was accessible to both Christians and non-Christians. We adapted this material for teens because, just like the adults in our community, they needed help understanding the gospel.*

The Gospel-Centered Life for Teens *is intended to help young adults understand how the gospel shapes every aspect of life and conduct. Colossians 1:6 says that the gospel is "continually bearing fruit and increasing" in and among us, even after we first believe it. How does that happen? Why is a continual rediscovery and application of the gospel so important? How will our personal growth and missional life be stunted if we don't grasp the gospel deeply? These are the questions that GCL for Teens seeks to answer.*

LEADER'S GUIDE

ABOUT THIS STUDY

The biggest advantage to *The Gospel-Centered Life for Teens* is its flexibility. It's appropriate for Sunday schools, youth groups, parachurch ministries, and campus ministries. It creates good dialogue among teenagers who are mature Christians as well as among new Christians and non-Christians. It can be led by an experienced small-group leader or by a high school student. And because the concepts are basic and biblical, it adapts easily to different cultural settings.

THE GOSPEL-CENTERED LIFE FOR TEENS IS IDEAL FOR:
- Youth pastors and youth leaders who are looking for content that "works" with diverse groups of people
- Students and campus ministers who are looking to live out the gospel on campus
- Christian teens who want to be more deeply formed around the gospel
- Missionaries who are looking for simple material to disciple teenagers

HOW THIS STUDY IS ORGANIZED

The Gospel-Centered Life for Teens contains nine lessons that are grouped around three themes. This *Leader's Guide* contains all the information needed to facilitate the group, as well as copies of the materials in the *Participant's Guide*.

What is the gospel?

LESSON 1: THE GOSPEL GRID

Everyone's life revolves around something, and we often label people accordingly. The point of this lesson is that God is meant to be our "center." Everything else will eventually fail us. Only a life that's centered on God will be meaningful, fulfilling, and satisfying. We will look at a simple diagram (the Cross Chart) that gives us a grid for seeing how to

Introduction 3

put the gospel at the center of our lives, and discover the only label that matters: "in Christ."

LESSON 2: PRETENDING

Each of us tends to "shrink the cross," which is to say that something is lacking in our understanding, appreciation, or application of Jesus's sacrifice for our sin. One way we do this is by pretending. Pretending minimizes sin by making ourselves out to be something we are not.

LESSON 3: PERFORMING

Performing is another way of "shrinking the cross" that minimizes God's holiness by reducing his standard to something we can meet, thereby meriting his favor. Both pretending and performing are rooted in an inadequate view of God's holiness and our identity.

②What does the gospel do in us?

LESSON 4: LAW & GOSPEL

Continue to think about how the gospel interacts with our lives, but now we turn to consider the gospel's relationship to the law. What is the law? Does God expect me to obey it? What is the purpose of the law? How does the law help me to believe the gospel? How does the gospel help me to obey the law?

LESSON 5: REPENTANCE

This lesson deals with repentance. In our culture, this usually sounds like a bad thing, but repentance is the norm for gospel-centered living. Becoming more aware of God's holiness and our sinfulness leads us to repent and believe the gospel of Jesus. Biblical repentance frees us from our own devices and makes a way for the power of the gospel to bear fruit in our lives.

LESSON 6: HEART IDOLATRY

The Christian walk consists of two repeated steps: repentance and faith. Turning our attention to the topic of faith, we focus on how we grow through believing the gospel. This week's goal is to take "believing the gospel" out of the abstract and make it concrete.

How does the gospel work through us?

LESSON 7: MISSION
The gospel is simultaneously at work in us and through us. Inwardly, our desires and motives are being changed as we repent and believe the gospel. As we experience Christ's love in this way, we are compelled to engage those around us with the same kind of redemptive love. God's grace brings renewal everywhere, in us and through us.

LESSON 8: FORGIVENESS
The gospel that works in us always works through us. It shows its power in our relationships and actions. One key way this happens is when we forgive others biblically.

LESSON 9: CONFLICT
Conflict is something we all experience (regularly), but often handle in very fleshly ways. The gospel gives us a pattern and a means to healthy conflict resolution.

HOW TO USE THIS STUDY

The Gospel-Centered Life for Teens is designed for small group study, although it is possible to work through the study independently or in a larger group. The tone of the material assumes a small-group format, because this is the setting we've found to be the most effective.

Each lesson is designed to take around 1 hour to complete. If your group has more time available, you can simply spend a little longer in the Discussion and Exercise sections. Our experience has shown that this content often creates deep and substantive conversation that can easily last longer than an hour. So plan accordingly, and be sure to honor the time commitment that your group has made.

Because *The Gospel-Centered Life for Teens* is designed as an introduction to the dynamics of gospel renewal, there is no outside work required by the participants. Each person should simply receive a copy of the Participant's Guide for the lesson at hand. The content will often stimulate further reflection over the following days, but no preparation is needed for subsequent lessons.

Likewise, it is not assumed that the group leader will be an expert theologian or long-standing Christian. Ample direction and content is provided in the Leader's Guide to help the leader facilitate the group's time together. The material also provides the content for the study, so there is no need for the group leader to try and "teach" the group. Just relax and guide a good conversation.

Each of these lessons follows a similar format including these elements…

BIBLE CONVERSATION
We want to start by talking about the Bible together. As the name suggests, this section is designed to stimulate your thinking and prepare you and your group for the ideas that will be presented in each lesson.

ARTICLE
The written articles are the primary source of the teaching content for each lesson. They are short, clear teachings of the concepts being presented in the lesson. Each week, your group will take a few minutes and read the article out loud together.

DISCUSSION
This section is where we communally process the concepts being taught in the article. Often the discussion will work in conjunction with the next section (exercise) to help flesh out the teaching and apply it to our lives in concrete ways.

EXERCISE
Each of the exercises in this study is designed to help you make practical applications of the concepts being taught, or help you understand the content at a deeper heart level. Be sure to allow enough time for your group to adequately work through and discuss the exercises as directed.

WRAP-UP
The wrap-up gives the leader the chance to answer any last minute questions, reinforce ideas, and most importantly spend a few minutes praying as a group.

WHAT TO EXPECT

EXPECT TO BE CHALLENGED...
most of us have reduced the gospel to something much less than it is. As you work through each lesson, expect your thinking about the gospel to be challenged and expanded.

EXPECT THE HOLY SPIRIT...
to be the one ultimately responsible for the growth of your group, and for the change in each person's life—including your own. Relax and trust him.

EXPECT YOUR GROUP'S AGENDA TO INCLUDE...
an open, give-and-take discussion of the article, the questions, and the exercises. Also expect times of prayer at each meeting.

EXPECT STRUGGLE...
and don't be surprised to find that your group is a mixture of enthusiasm, hope, and honesty, along with indifference, anxiety, skepticism, guilt, and covering up. We are all people who really need Jesus every day. So expect your group to be made up of people who wrestle with sin and have problems—people just like yourself!

EXPECT A GROUP LEADER...
who desires to serve you, but who also needs Jesus as much as you do. No leader should be put on a pedestal, so expect that your group leader will have the freedom to share openly about his or her own weaknesses, struggles, and sins.

GOSPEL OVERVIEW

The study you are about to begin aims to help you live a "gospel-centered" life. The obvious question is, What exactly is "the gospel"? That's a question we should clear up before going any further. Though many people are familiar with the word *gospel*, they're often fuzzy about its content.

Many popular "gospel presentations" distill the gospel message down to three or four core principles. These simple summaries can be very helpful. But a richer way to understand the gospel is as a *story*—the true Story that speaks to our purest aspirations and deepest longings. This Great Story has four chapters.

CREATION: THE WORLD WE WERE MADE FOR

The Story begins, not with us, but with God. Deep down, we have a sense that this is true. We sense that we are important—that there is something dignified, majestic, and eternal about humanity. But we also know that we are not ultimate. Something (or Someone) greater than us exists.

The Bible tells us that this Someone is the one infinite, eternal, and unchanging God who created all things out of nothing (Genesis 1:1–31). This one God exists in three persons—Father, Son, and Holy Spirit (Matthew 28:19). Because God is Triune in his being, he wasn't motivated to create the world because he *needed* something—be it relationship, worship, or glory. Rather, he created out of the overflow of his perfection—his own love, goodness, and glory. God made human beings in his image (Genesis 1:27), which is what gives us our dignity and value. He also made us *human*, which means we are created beings, dependent on our Creator. We were made to worship, enjoy, love, and serve him, not ourselves.

In God's original creation, everything was good. The world existed in perfect peace, stability, harmony, and wholeness.

FALL: THE CORRUPTION OF EVERYTHING

God created us to worship, enjoy, love, and serve him. But rather than live under God's authority, humanity turned away from God in sinful rebellion (Genesis 3:1–7; Isaiah 53:6). Our defection plunged the whole world into the darkness and chaos of sin. Though vestiges of good remain, the wholeness and harmony of God's original creation is shattered.

As a result, all human beings are sinners by nature and by choice (Ephesians 2:1–3). We often excuse our sin by claiming that we're "not that bad"—after all, we can always find someone worse than we are! But this evasion only reveals our shallow and superficial view of sin. Sin is not primarily an *action*; it's a *disposition*. It's our soul's aversion to God. Sin is manifested in our pride, our selfishness, our independence, and our lack of love for God and others. Sometimes sin is very obvious and external; other times it's hidden and internal. But "all have sinned and fall short of the glory of God" (Romans 3:23).

Sin brings two drastic consequences into our lives. First, *sin enslaves us* (Romans 6:17–18). When we turn *from* God, we turn *to* other things to find our life, our identity, our meaning, and our happiness. These things become substitute gods—what the Bible calls idols—and they soon enslave us, demanding our time, our energy, our loyalty, our money—everything we are and have. They begin to rule over our lives and hearts. This is why the Bible describes sin as something that "masters" us (Romans 6:14 NIV). Sin causes us to "serve created things rather than the Creator" (Romans 1:25 NIV).

Second, *sin brings condemnation*. We're not just enslaved by our sin; we're *guilty* because of it. We stand condemned before the Judge of heaven and earth. "The wages of sin is death" (Romans 6:23). We are under a death sentence for our cosmic treason against the holiness and justice of God. His righteous anger toward sin stands over us (Nahum 1:2; John 3:36).

REDEMPTION: JESUS COMES TO SAVE US

Every good story has a hero. And the hero of the Gospel Story is Jesus. Humanity needs a Savior, a Redeemer, a Deliverer to free us from the bondage and condemnation of sin and to restore the world to its original good. This Rescuer must be *truly human* in order to pay the debt we owe to God. But he can't be *merely human* because he must conquer sin. We need a Substitute—one who can live the life of obedience we've failed to live, and who can stand in our place to bear the punishment we deserve for our disobedience and sin.

This is why God sent Jesus into the world to be our substitute (1 John 4:14). The Bible teaches that Jesus was fully God—the second person of the Trinity—and also fully human. He was born to a human mother, lived a real flesh-and-blood existence, and died a brutal death on a Roman cross outside Jerusalem. Jesus lived a life of perfect obedience to God (Hebrews 4:15), making him the only person in history who did not deserve judgment. But on the cross, he took our place, dying for our sin. He received the condemnation and death we deserve so that, when we put our trust in him, we can receive the blessing and life he deserves (2 Corinthians 5:21).

Not only did Jesus die in our place, he rose from death, displaying his victory over sin, death, and hell. His resurrection is a decisive event in history; the Bible calls it the "first fruits"—the initial evidence—of the cosmic renewal God is bringing (1 Corinthians 15:20–28). One of the greatest promises in the Bible is Revelation 21:5: "Behold, I am making all things new." All that was lost, broken, and corrupted in the fall will ultimately be put right. Redemption doesn't simply mean the salvation of individual souls; it means the restoring of the whole creation back to its original good.

A NEW PEOPLE: THE STORY CONTINUES

So how do we become a part of the story? How do we experience God's salvation personally and become agents of his redemption in the world?

By faith or trust (Ephesians 2:8–9). What does that mean? We trust a taxi driver when we count on him to get us to our destination. We trust a doctor when we agree with her diagnosis and entrust ourselves to her care. And we trust in Jesus Christ when we admit our sin, receive his gracious forgiveness, and rest entirely in Jesus for our acceptance before God. Faith is like getting in the taxi. It's like going under the surgeon's knife. It's a restful, whole-hearted commitment of the self to Jesus (Psalm 31:14–15). This is what it means to believe the gospel.

When we trust in Jesus, we are released from sin's condemnation *and* from its bondage. We are free to say "no" to sin and "yes" to God. We are free to die to ourselves and live for Christ and his purposes. We are free to work for justice in the world. We are free to stop living for our own glory and start living for the glory of God (1 Corinthians 10:31). We are free to love God and others in the way we live, which is the particular focus of this study.

God has promised that Jesus will return to finally judge sin and make all things new. Until then, he is gathering to himself a people "from every nation, tribe, people and language" (Revelation 7:9 NIV). As part of that called-and-sent people, we have the privilege of joining him in his mission (Matthew 28:18–20) as individuals and as part of his spiritual family. By grace, we can enjoy God, live life for his glory, serve humanity, and make his gospel known to others through our words and actions.

This is the good news—the True Story—of the gospel.

lesson

THE GOSPEL GRID

BIG IDEA

Everyone's life revolves around something, and we often label people accordingly. The point of this lesson is that God is meant to be our "center." Everything else will eventually fail us. Only a life that's centered on God will be meaningful, fulfilling, and satisfying. We will look at a simple diagram (the Cross Chart) that gives us a grid for seeing how to put the gospel at the center of our lives, and discover the only label that matters: "in Christ."

LESSON OVERVIEW

I. BIBLE CONVERSATION	Read and talk about the passage(s) [10 min]
II. ARTICLE	Read *The Gospel Grid* together [10 min]
III. DISCUSSION	Process concepts together [15 min]
IV. EXERCISE	Apply the concepts using a specific exercise [15 min]
V. WRAP-UP	Final thoughts and prayer [5 min]

BIBLE CONVERSATION *10 minutes*

We are focusing on two major concepts in this lesson: who God is and who we are. The passages highlight the holiness of God and the depth of our sinfulness. The goal here is not to say everything there is to say about these ideas. The goal is simply to get the conversation going in a way

13

that establishes a biblical foundation for the concepts, which will unfold throughout the discussion.

SETUP We are going to talk about two concepts: how we view God and how we view ourselves. These concepts lay the foundation for understanding ourselves and understanding why the gospel is so important. When it comes to the way we view God, there tends to be a range of opinions. Some people have a very high view of God, to the point that he is totally "other" and uninvolved in daily life. Others have a very personal view of God, to the point that he is so much like a best friend that his holiness is neglected. The same is true for the way we view ourselves: the spectrum ranges from the idea that people are basically good to basically bad. Let's see where we land on each of these questions.

ASK Which end of the spectrum do you lean toward when it comes to God: is he majestic and distant, or so personal that you don't think much about his holiness?

ASK Which thought best represents your view of people: basically good or basically bad?

Let's look at two Bible passages that highlight these two concepts. The main two questions to ask as we read these verses are (1) What does this say about God? and (2) What does this say about me?

READ The first passage is Isaiah 55:6–9. *(Have someone read Isaiah 55:6–9 out loud.)*

ASK What is your initial reaction to this passage?
What stands out to you? What does this say about God—and us?

READ The next passage is Jeremiah 17:9–10. *(Have someone read Jeremiah 17:9–10 out loud.)*

ASK What is your initial reaction to this passage? What stands out to you?

What does this say about God—and us?

TRANSITION TO ARTICLE These passages introduce us to the biblical view of God's holiness and our sinfulness. To get a more focused understanding of these ideas, let's read this article together. We are going to read it aloud, taking turns at the paragraph breaks. Then I have some discussion questions that will help us process it together.

ARTICLE *10 minutes*

This lesson assumes a basic familiarity with the gospel. If that's a generous assumption for your group, consider reading through the "Gospel Overview" in the Front Matter together before you progress through the reading for this lesson. It will add about ten minutes to your study, but it will be well worth it.

The point of reading an article together is twofold: (1) To explain key concepts so everyone in your group has a common understanding and language, and (2) to provide a focus for conversation. Remember, we are trying to help your group learn how to talk about the gospel in relation to their actual lives. In many cases, people do not talk about the gospel or their lives because they simply don't have much to say. The article gives them content to talk about.

Ask your group to turn to the article The Gospel Grid in their Participant's Guide and read it aloud together, taking turns at the paragraph breaks.

TRANSITION TO DISCUSSION There is some good stuff here. So let's read this article together and see what it says about these issues. As we do, I want to focus on understanding the concepts and relating them to our lives. If there is something you don't get, ask questions so we can talk it through together. I have some questions that will help us dig a little deeper as we go.

DISCUSSION *15 minutes*

These questions are aimed at helping the group talk through the Cross Chart. Those who do not understand it will be able to work it out in community, and those who "get it" will benefit from learning how to articulate it. You may want to ask follow-up questions as you go.

1. Let's recap the main ideas from the article.

ASK   What are some problems with being centered on something other than the gospel?

ASK   What two things are to be growing as we mature in faith? What does that mean? How do we do that?

ASK   What "label" do we get when we believe the gospel?

2. Let's personalize these concepts a bit.

ASK   What are some of the labels people use at your school?

ASK   What would people who know you say your life revolves around?

ASK   What sounds attractive to you about centering your life on God? How would you even do that?

ASK   What makes you feel unsure about centering your life on God?

TRANSITION TO EXERCISE   This is really good. We are talking about some significant things that we will continue to explore in the next two sessions. I want to end with an exercise that will help us apply what we have been talking about to a specific area we all deal with.

EXERCISE 15 minutes

*The point of this exercise is to apply the Cross Chart to a specific issue that will help everyone see (1) how their sin is rooted in a small view of the gospel and (2) how a big view of the gospel helps us overcome sin. **Note:** Not everyone needs to answer every question aloud, but try to draw out as many people as you can throughout the exercise.*

SETUP   Let's take the issue of judging others. Judging others means labeling them, looking down on them, or thinking you are better than them in some way. We all do this in various ways. So let's start by quickly brainstorming a list of ways we judge others. Even if it's just the little everyday judgments we make, what are some specific ways we judge others?

(Write down a list of ways we judge others based on the group's answers.) So that's how we judge others. Let's talk about why we do this.

ASK   What are the reasons we judge others? Let's brainstorm another list together.

ASK   How do these reasons reflect a small view of God's holiness?

ASK   How do these reasons reflect a small view of our own sin?

Okay, let's get personal. Think of a specific person in your life that you are often judgmental toward.

ASK   How would a bigger view of God's holiness affect that relationship?

ASK   How would a bigger view of your sin affect that relationship?

TRANSITION TO WRAP-UP   This has been really good. Thanks for sharing. We will be talking about the Cross Chart the next two weeks as well, and doing exercises like this one to help us make it practical. Before we wrap up, does anyone have any lingering questions or comments? Okay, let's spend a few minutes praying together. If some of you want to pray, I will close in a few minutes.

WRAP-UP *5 minutes*

Questions, comments, prayer.

lesson

1

ARTICLE 1

THE GOSPEL GRID

What does your life revolve around? What people, interests, or pursuits consume your time and attention?

Everyone's life has a center. Think of the solar system: the sun is the center, and everything else revolves around it. Your life is kind of like that. There's something at the center that everything else tends to revolve around.

For some of us, the center is our grades. For others, it's sports. For others, it's music. For others, it's boyfriends or girlfriends or relationships. Whatever it is, that "center" also tends to give us a sense of identity. If you're the pretty girl who gets noticed by boys, you probably enjoy that sense of acceptance. If you're the athletic kid who's good at sports, you probably enjoy the attention and affirmation. If you're the smart kid who does well in school, it feels good to get noticed for your intelligence.

Sometimes other people try to define a "center" for us by labeling us with a certain identity. Maybe you've been called "the nerd" or "the slut" or "the misfit" or "the religious kid." Maybe you've labeled other people in these sorts of ways too. There are some labels we like because they give us a sense of being acceptable: "I'm smart (or kind or funny), and therefore I belong." And there are other labels we don't want, because we think we are better than that: "Some people are arrogant or annoying or losers, but I am not like that." We're busy either embracing the labels people give us, or working hard to reject them and forge a *different* identity.

What's at the center of your life? What's defining your identity?

The point of this lesson, and of this whole study, is that God is meant to be your center. He's the only thing in the universe with the "gravitational pull" to keep your life in balance. Anything else that you put at the center of your life will eventually fail you. Only a life that's centered on God will be meaningful, fulfilling, and satisfying.

We're going to be talking about this idea of a God-centered life for the next few weeks. But as a starting point, we need to understand some basic truths about God, about ourselves, and about the gospel. Understanding the gospel will help you see why it's so hard to live a God-centered life on your own and how much you need a Savior—not only to get to heaven (an important goal!), but also to live life to the fullest right now.

The word *gospel* means "good news." It is the good news that God saves sinners through the life, death, and resurrection of Jesus. The following diagram is a helpful illustration of what it means to center our life on this good news:

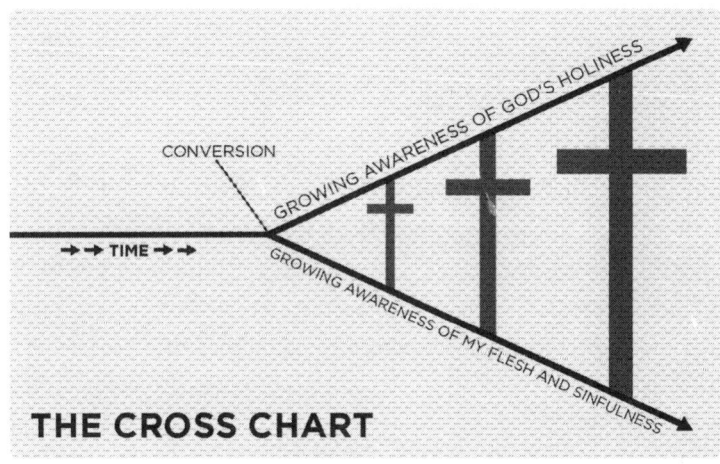

In order to become a Christian, I must become aware of the gap that exists between who God is and who I am. God is holy, which means "set apart." God is completely good, loving, and wise—perfect in all of his ways (Deuteronomy 32:3–4). We, on the other hand, are not. The real reason we don't center our lives on God is that we don't want to. We want to go our own way, not God's way. That's what the Bible calls "sin." So it's not just that we're a little bit different from God; we're in a different category altogether. We have never been perfect in all of our ways for even one day. We are sinful. We are naturally bent to think and act in ways that are not like God. That means there is a huge gap between God and us.

But here's the good news: Jesus Christ came to bridge the gap between God and us. He came to live and die in our place, as our substitute. As Tim Keller puts it, "He lived the life we should have lived, and died the death we deserved to die because of our sin, so that God could accept us."

Being a Christian means turning from going our own way (our sin) and trusting in Jesus as our substitute. It means that we follow the ABC's of faith:

- A) Admit our sin before a holy God—that we are guilty and in need of salvation,
- B) Believe in Jesus—not just intellectually, but with our heart and life, and
- C) Confess Jesus as Lord—turn our lives over to him and become his disciples, his followers.

As the Cross Chart shows, when we put our trust in Jesus, he becomes the center of our lives. He now defines our identity. The Bible calls this new identity being "in Christ." The most important thing about us—the thing that defines us—is not grades or sports or boys or girls or music or coolness, but Jesus! He is the gravitational pull that keeps our life on the right course.

The more we grow in our awareness of who God is and who we really are, the more we experience our new life in Christ. As we read the Bible, as we experience the work of God's Spirit in us, and as we live in community with God's people, the extent of God's holiness and the extent of our sinfulness become increasingly clear. It is not that God is becoming more holy or that we are becoming more sinful. It's just that our awareness of both is growing. We are increasingly seeing God as he actually is (Isaiah 55:6–9) and ourselves as we actually are (Jeremiah 17:9–10). And we are becoming more "centered" in our new identity in Jesus. That's why it's important to see the gospel as both the entry point into the Christian life and the pathway of the Christian life.

As our understanding of God's holiness and our sinfulness grows, something else also grows: our appreciation and love for Jesus. The Holy Spirit makes Jesus's life, death, and resurrection increasingly real and powerful to us. We realize more and more that the labels we want don't come anywhere close to the holiness of God. And we realize that we are not better than other people—no matter what label we may have given them. Like us, they are also sinners who need to be saved by Jesus.

A gospel-centered life means a life that's centered on the only category that really matters: "in Christ."

lesson

1

EXERCISE 1

JUDGING OTHERS

One way to see the value of the Cross Chart is to apply it to a specific area where people commonly struggle. Judging others is something we all do in big and small ways. We judge others when we label them, look down on them, or think we are better than them in some way.

As a group, brainstorm about some of the specific ways we judge people, or feel judged. The questions below will help you see the connection between judging others and your view of the gospel.

1. Have you ever felt judged? How and why?

2. What are the specific ways you have judged/labeled others?

3. Why do we judge others? What reasons do we give for doing this?

4. How do these reasons reflect a small view of God's holiness?

5. How do these reasons reflect a small view of our own sin?

6. Think of a specific person or group of people in your life that you often feel judged by.

    a. How would a bigger view of God's holiness affect that relationship?

    b. How would a bigger view of our sinfulness affect that relationship?

PRETENDING

lesson **LEADER'S GUIDE**

BIG IDEA

This lesson deals with one of the ways we "shrink the cross," which is just a way of saying that something is lacking in our understanding, appreciation, or application of Jesus's sacrifice for our sin. This happens in two main ways: pretending and performing. This week is about pretending, and lesson three is about performing. Both pretending and performing keep us from living a God-centered life. Pretending minimizes sin by making ourselves out to be something we are not. Gospel growth comes as we learn to confess our sin instead of try to cover it up.

LESSON OVERVIEW

I. BIBLE CONVERSATION	Read and talk about the passage(s) [10 min]	
II. ARTICLE	Read *Shrinking the Cross: Pretending* together [10 min]	
III. DISCUSSION	Process concepts together [15 min]	
IV. EXERCISE	Apply the concepts using a specific exercise [15 min]	
V. WRAP-UP	Final thoughts and prayer [5 min]	

BIBLE CONVERSATION *10 minutes*

Mark 2:13–17 begins with Jesus calling Levi to follow him. In the eyes of the religious leaders (Pharisees), Levi was a hated tax collector and condemned sinner. When the Pharisees see Jesus dining with Levi and his friends, they cannot imagine why he would associate with such sinners. Then the point of the story comes in vs. 17: Jesus came to save sinners, which is everyone, but those who don't see themselves as sinners don't receive Jesus and what he came to bring.

This is a short story, so take your time and put yourselves in the shoes of the various characters. Let the group wrestle with what Jesus could be saying in verse 17. It's always better if they arrive at the meaning through conversation and discovery, as opposed to someone just telling them what it means.

SETUP   We are going to read a story in Mark 2. This takes place when Jesus was beginning his ministry. One of the first things Jesus did was gather twelve men to be his disciples, or students. This story is about one of those guys, named Levi.

READ   Mark 2:13-17 *(Have someone read Mark 2:13-17 aloud.)*

ASK   Which character do you identify most with? As we read, did you see yourself as Levi, or more like the Pharisees? Why?

ASK   Why are the Pharisees so bothered by what Jesus is doing?

ASK   In verse 17:

- What does Jesus mean by "well" and "sick"?
- Are some people really good all the time (i.e. righteous), and therefore do not need Jesus?
- If not, then why would Jesus say this?

TRANSITION TO ARTICLE   This story shows us how important it is to have a right view of ourselves and the dangers of thinking we are better than we really are. The article we are going to read calls this "pretending." Let's read it together and then we can talk about how this applies to us.

ARTICLE *10 minutes*

Some people feel that reading an article feels too formal. We agree, but we have also seen the benefit of getting everyone on the same page with a common language. The content in the article acts as kindling to get the conversation going. Without it, you will get a bunch of smoke.

Ask your group to turn to the article *Shrinking the Cross: Pretending* in their Participant's Guide and read it aloud together, taking turns at the paragraph breaks.

DISCUSSION *15 minutes*

ASK What are some ways that we "work hard to put forward an image that people will like"?

ASK How do you feel about seeing the depths of your brokenness, or being seen by others in this way? Are you hesitant or willing? Why?

ASK Do you like to be convicted of your sin or does it feel like a "crushing weight"?

Let's do a little experiment:

ASK In the past week, how often have you thought, said, or done something that would be considered sinful (unpleasing to God)? Let's just get a quick show of hands. Who would say 0-10 times, 10-20, 20-50, 50-100, 100+?

ASK Okay, how many times would you say that you actually confessed sin to God (admitted your sin and asked for forgiveness)? Who would say 0-10 times, 10-20, 20-50, 50-100, 100+?

SAY It looks like we all have done lots of things worth confessing, yet most of us have not actually confessed very much.

ASK Why do you think that is?

TRANSITION TO EXERCISE It's eye opening to realize how prone we are to pretending, and how that keeps us from experiencing the gospel's power in our lives. Pretending comes so naturally to us that it is hard to know when we are doing it. Our exercise this week helps us identify the subtle ways that we minimize our sin.

EXERCISE *15 minutes*

SETUP   Sometimes it is hard to identify the ways we minimize and justify our sin (bottom line of the chart). Take a look at the supplement Six Ways of Minimizing Sin in your Participant's Guide.

Take a few minutes to read each description, and then pick one or two that you most identify with.

ASK   Which one of these do you see yourself doing most often? *(Ask everyone to share the one they relate to the most.)*

ASK   Can anyone share a recent example of a time when you minimized or justified your sin in one of these ways?

ASK   When we do these things, how does it keep us from experiencing the power of the gospel in our lives (forgiveness, healing, growth)?

TRANSITION TO WRAP-UP   This has been really good. Thanks for sharing. We are going to continue working through these concepts over the next few weeks. Before we wrap up, does anyone have any lingering questions or comments? . . . Okay, let's spend a few minutes praying together. This would be good time to confess our sin together. I'll get us started, and then after some others pray, I will close us.

WRAP-UP *5 minutes*

Questions, comments, prayer.

lesson 2 — ARTICLE

SHRINKING THE CROSS: PRETENDING

What if you were surfing the Internet one day and came across a website that kept an updated log of all your thoughts and actions? How would you feel upon discovering this public record of your private life?

We all have two versions of ourselves. There is the image we portray to those around us, and there is the real us, when nobody is looking. The reason we all have two versions is because deep down we believe that if people knew the real us, they would reject us, or at least avoid us. So we work hard to put forward an image that people will like.

We do the same thing with God. In the beginning of the biblical story (Genesis 1-2), God made a beautiful world, and he made people to enjoy that world. There was no shame or pride or suffering, just joy and peace. Sadly, things didn't stay that way. Adam and Eve, the first man and woman, were deceived into thinking that they could become like God (Genesis 3). So they did the one thing God told them not to do. What followed was a sad unraveling of the world God had made for them. Instead of joy and peace, they felt shame and fear, and then quickly turned on each other.

All of this is wrapped up in what the Bible calls sin: going our way not God's way, looking for life apart from God and getting death instead. By trying to be God, Adam and Eve broke our world. And that's the world we live in today—broken by sin. We see it every day in the news, at school, in our families. And we see it in ourselves.

We were made to be known as we really are, by God and by others. This is what the author of Genesis was trying to convey by telling us that Adam and Eve "were both naked and were not ashamed" (Genesis 2:25). They didn't put up a front; they didn't spin the truth; they never tried to compensate for insecurity and fear. They didn't even know they were naked because there had never been any other reality. This is almost impossible for us to imagine. I mean, if you were walking around school and suddenly realized that you did not have clothes on, you would freak out. You would be naked and totally ashamed. We were made for unhindered friendship with God and others, but sin has ruined everything.

When Adam and Eve ate the fruit God told them not to eat, "the eyes of both were opened, and they knew that they were naked. And they sewed fig leaves together and made themselves loincloths" (Genesis 3:7). Shame is the feeling that you have been exposed, and therefore that you do not belong. This is how they felt. Their nakedness was suddenly shameful and they felt exposed. So they ran for cover. This is the aftermath of the fall: we feel shame, and we are constantly trying to cover our shame so no one will see. As a result, the power of the cross shrinks in our life.

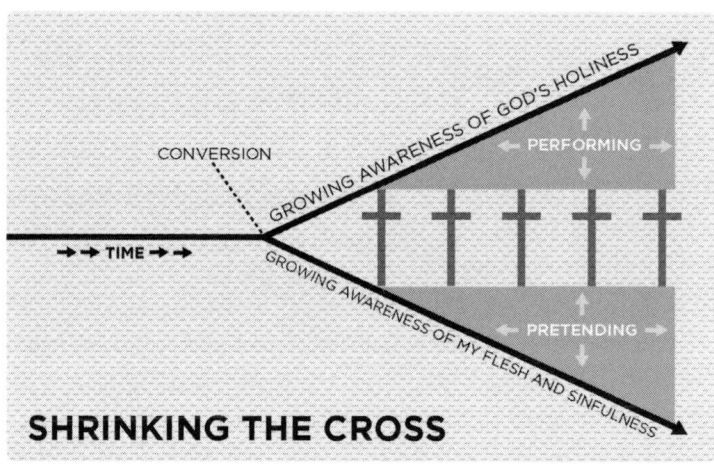

When we become more aware of our sinfulness (the bottom line), we feel exposed and ashamed. So we compensate by pretending that we're better than we really are. Pretending can take many forms: dishonesty ("I'm not that bad"), comparison ("I'm not as bad as those people"), excuse making ("I'm not really that way"), and trying to make ourselves right with God ("Here are all the good things I've done"). Because we don't want to admit how sinful we really are, we spin the truth in our favor.

We all carry shame in us. We may not always be conscious of it, might not be able to name it, but it is there. And we have developed so many ways to hide it. For instance, if you are the kind of person who is defensive and usually blames others or justifies your actions, that is a way to protect yourself against exposure. If you are hypercritical of everything, that is a way of turning the attention elsewhere. If you are given excessively to pleasure or fantasy, those are often just ways of trying to deaden yourself to your feelings of shame. None of it works though. The more we try to hide, the greater our shame becomes, and the worse we feel (Psalm 32:3-4). When we do not deal with shame, it deals with us.

Jesus came to redeem the real us, not the person we pretend to be. So how do we stop pretending?

First, we have to admit how much we need God. One of the ways we cover our sin is by pretending that the solution is something other than God. We often think: *If I just had that relationship or GPA, or group of friends, or body, or thing—something to cover up my brokenness—then everything would be okay.* But it wouldn't be okay because the world or people can't give us what we truly need. It would be foolish to only take painkillers when you have cancer. You might feel better, but you wouldn't deal with the real problem. All the things that you think will make you "okay" are just painkillers. God wants to heal the real you.

Second, if we want to experience the power of the gospel in our lives, we have to bring our real lives into the light. That begins by confessing our sin to God. After Adam and Eve tried to cover their sin, God came looking for them. He said, "Adam, where are you?" . . . "What is this that you have done?" (Genesis 3:9,13). Why did he say that if already knew? Because he wants to restore us, not condemn us.

Confession is not a formula. It's about restoring a relationship. That is really the only way you can deal with your shame. In other words, you don't confess your way out of shame. Shame is overcome when someone knows everything about you and still accepts and loves you. God comes to us and says, "Where are you?" … "What have you done?" because he is inviting us into the kind of relationship that will cover our shame.

Here are three "steps" to bring the real you into the light:

1. **Turn to God.** We often turn to others to get approval or to place blame, but that is just looking for cover. Turning to God means we are looking for forgiveness.

2. **Be honest.** Get it all out there with God. Sometimes we just talk about the actions, but not the heart motives behind our actions. We give God 90 percent of the story, but we withhold the really dark stuff, the things that are too shameful to say, or the things we think God cannot forgive. Being honest about the last 10 percent is really hard work, but that is where the shame lives.

3. **Hide in God.** Adam and Eve made clothes to cover their nakedness, but when they confessed their sin to God, he made new clothes for them (Genesis 3:21). This is what God does for us in Christ. He clothes us with his goodness and his right actions (i.e. his righteousness) so that we don't have to hide behind the pretend version of ourselves. Our lives are "hidden with Christ in God" (Colossians 3:3).

Sin is not just doing bad things. It is trying to find life apart from God. It's centering our lives on something (anything!) except God. The good news is that Jesus died for the helpless and the ungodly (Romans 5:6). He came to redeem the real us, but when we pretend that we're not broken or thirsty, we short-circuit the work of his grace in our lives (Luke 5:29-39; 7:39-47). Getting honest about who we really are—and all the ways we are trying to pretend we're better than that—opens up the flow of God's grace in our lives.

lesson

EXERCISE 2

SIX WAYS OF MINIMIZING SIN

DEFENDING

I find it difficult to receive feedback about mistakes, weaknesses, or sin. When people (e.g., parents, teachers, friends) try to talk to me about them, my tendency is to explain things away, compare myself to someone who is acting worse than me, and/or justify my decisions. As a result, I don't often really "hear" any feedback about difficult things in my life.

FAKING

I try to keep up appearances and maintain my image—whatever person I am hoping that others will think I am. Most of what I say and do is motivated by what I think others think of me. As a result, not many people know the real me. (I may not even know the real me.)

HIDING

I try to cover up as much as I can about my life, especially the "bad stuff." This is different from faking, in that faking is about impressing. Hiding is more about shame. I don't think people will accept or love the real me.

EXAGGERATING

Sometimes I pretend to others that I'm better than I really am. I often "stretch" a story to make my life seem better than it is, or to show how I am better than others in some way. I exaggerate to keep up an impression that I am a great person.

BLAMING

I am quick to blame others for my circumstances or my actions. I have a difficult time "owning" anything bad that I have done or my part in a fight. Sometimes that's because I really don't think anything is my fault (pride) and sometimes it's because I don't want to be rejected (fear).

DOWNPLAYING

I tend to ignore the bad stuff that I do or the bad things that have happened to me. As a result, I don't deal with unhealthy habits, relationship problems, and tough circumstances. Then everything builds up to the point where I'm really overwhelmed.

lesson

PERFORMING

BIG IDEA

Last week we talked about one way we shrink the gospel (pretending), and how to get centered on God and the good news of the gospel through confession. In this lesson, we will talk about another way we shrink the cross (performing), and how to get centered on God and his gospel through believing. This lesson turns our attention to what remedies God has given in the gospel to keep us from shrinking the cross and depending on our own effort.

LESSON OVERVIEW

I. BIBLE CONVERSATION	Read and talk about the passage(s) [15 min]
II. ARTICLE	Read *Shrinking the Cross: Performing* together [10 min]
III. DISCUSSION	Process concepts together [5 min]
IV. EXERCISE	Apply the concepts using a specific exercise [25 min]
V. WRAP-UP	Final thoughts and prayer [5 min]

BIBLE CONVERSATION *15 minutes*

Second Peter 1:1–8 establishes a biblical foundation for the concepts in this lesson. Warning: this is more like an exercise that poses as a discussion. You need to understand the goal if you want to lead the conversation in the right direction. In this text, Peter says we have everything we need for life and godliness (vv. 3–4). Then he proceeds to list a bunch of things we should be doing in light of this reality (vv. 5–8). You are going to stop reading after verse 8 and ask the group how they are doing according to this list. Most people will express struggle. Then you will ask them why this is such a challenge. They will likely list all kinds of very legitimate reasons and explanations. What they are not likely to identify as the problem is the exact thing Peter does identify in verse 9, namely, that they have drifted away from the gospel. It's a punch line; so don't give it away until you get there! This is one of those things that need to smack us in the face.

SETUP We are going to look at a great passage but before we do, let me ask you a question: when you envision the kind of person you want to be spiritually, what kinds of things do you see? *(Make a list of the qualities and actions mentioned.)*

TRANSITION TO PASSAGE This is a great list. Perhaps we could summarize our desires as "being fruitful and effective in our faith." I use those words because those are the words Peter uses in the passage we are going to read. Peter lays out a set of instructions for the Christian life. It's like a progression of spiritual maturity.

READ Let's look at it together. It is in 2 Peter 1 *(Have someone read 2 Peter 1:3–8 aloud.)*

ASK Peter says in verse 8 that if we do the things mentioned in verses 5–7, we will be fruitful and effective in our faith (which is really what we all want). How do you think you are doing according to this list? If you compared yourself to the qualities listed here, how would you rate your progress?

ASK Why is it difficult sometimes to grow spiritually? What challenges do you face when it comes to doing the things Peter lists or becoming the person you want to be? *(Make a list of the reasons people give.)*

ASK I would say many of the same things. These are all real challenges. But Peter identifies something else altogether. Read verse 9. *(Have someone read the verse aloud.)* According to Peter, what is the real reason we don't grow spiritually?

Leader's Guide

TRANSITION TO ARTICLE This goes back to what we talked about in the first lesson— the gospel is not just the entry point, but also the pathway of spiritual life. The article we're about to read is going to explain further how the gospel changes us.

ARTICLE *10 minutes*

Ask your group to turn to the article *Shrinking the Cross: Performing* in their Participant's Guide and read it aloud together, taking turns at the paragraph breaks.

DISCUSSION *5 minutes*

There isn't really a formal discussion for this article because the concepts are worked out in the exercise. However, it is a good idea to make sure people understand the article. You may just ask if anyone has any clarifying questions, or you may ask a few questions to see if people are tracking with the article. Either way, once you feel good about it, go to the exercise. It will take some time.

TRANSITION TO EXERCISE There are some really important concepts in this article that we need to personalize, so I want to take some time to do this exercise. It will help us understand how we can apply the gospel more effectively to our lives.

EXERCISE *25 minutes*

1. Turn to the Orphans vs. Children exercise

2. Read aloud the paragraph at the top.

3. Give people a few minutes to complete the chart individually.

4. Sharing (Left Side): I want everyone to share what he or she recognized about himself or herself. Starting with the left side, let's go around the room and share our top two or three "orphan" tendencies.

Lesson 3   35

After everyone has shared, pick the three or four most common bullet points for your group. For each one, ask these questions:

ASK   How does feeling this way affect how we relate to God and others?

ASK   How does this tendency reveal a fundamental unbelief in the truths of the gospel (specifically passive righteousness)?

5. Sharing (Right Side): Now let's go around the room starting with the right side. I'd like each of you to share the two or three ways that you want to see God change you? (*You can share ways you have seen God at work in your life, or perhaps you are just drawn to a few of the "children" characteristics and really want God to work in you in those ways.*)

After everyone has shared, pick the three or four most common bullet points for your group. For each one, ask these questions:

ASK   How would this change the way you relate to God and to others?

ASK   How does knowing God as our Father and that we are forgiven in Christ empower us to grow in this way?

WRAP-UP *5 minutes*

Questions, comments, prayer.

lesson

ARTICLE 3

SHRINKING THE CROSS: PERFORMING

Everyone is trying to fit in somewhere. Even those who say they don't care if they fit in are usually trying to fit in with the crowd that doesn't care. Think about it: Why do we wear the clothes we wear? Why do we talk the way we do– using particular words and phrases? Did you ever say something you don't mean just to get attention? I have. Have you ever done something just because people you wanted to hang out with were doing it? I have. Have you ever exaggerated your good points? And made fun of others who didn't fit in? If we are honest, we say and do these kinds of things because we want to fit in.

But have you ever thought about why we want to fit in, why *everyone* wants to fit in? The reason we want acceptance, approval, and significance is because God designed us to find these things in him. The problem is that because sin separated us from God, we try to get these things elsewhere.

One of the most important words in the Bible has to do with this idea of belonging. It's the word, *righteousness*. You'll find it in almost every book of the New Testament. I know it sounds like a boring, religious word, but it's something we all want and it affects what we say and do every day.

Righteousness means to be in right standing. So whatever gives you a sense of worth or belonging is a source of righteousness. It could be your intellect, athleticism, looks, humor, boyfriend or girlfriend, taste in music, or being different.

Everywhere you go there are certain values and behaviors that keep you in right standing—with the courts, your family, your school, and even your group of friends. In each of these areas of life, if you live up to the standards, then you will find validation and approval. You'll fit in.

That's why growing in our awareness of God's holiness is challenging. It means coming face-to-face with God's standards—his perfect character and his commandments. Think about how inadequate you feel when you are around someone who is good at everything. Then add to that the feeling you get when someone has super high expectations of you. Now multiply that by a jillion, and you are still not even close to the perfect character and commands of God.

We want to measure up; we want to be good enough; but the simple truth is that we fall way short of God's standards. And deep down we know we don't measure up. That's why there is such a frantic search in our world for at least being in right standing with some group of people. But that's a poor substitute for what we really need—right standing before God. Without getting right with God, the approval and sense of belonging we get from others will never be enough for us. But no matter how hard any of us try, we can never measure up to God's standards of holiness. We are broken by sin. Ever since Adam and Eve, no one has been able to stop sinning on their own. We all inherited their desire to go their way, not God's way.

We are not in right standing with God at all. Instead we are in the worst standing possible and deserve God's wrath (Romans 1:18). That's bad news. But it's the terrible news of God's wrath against sin that makes the gospel of Jesus such good news. The gospel gives us right standing with God. Let's look at the Cross Chart again to understand how this works.

LEADER'S GUIDE

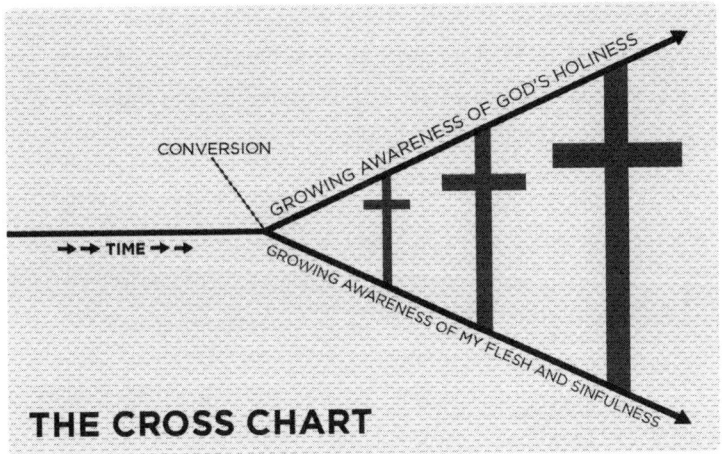

THE CROSS CHART

The huge gap between God and us means we could never be good enough to fit in with God. "For Christ also suffered once for sins, the righteous for the unrighteous, that he might bring us to God" (1 Peter 3:18). The essence of what it means to be a Christian is to be united with Christ through faith. That means that when God looks at us, he sees Christ in our place. He sees the sacrifice of Jesus for sin, and credits all our sin to his account. He also sees the perfect obedience of Jesus and credits his righteousness to our account. God is pleased with us because he is pleased with his Son Jesus.

The apostle Paul put it this way, "He made him [Jesus] to be sin who knew no sin, so that in him we might become the righteousness of God (2 Corinthians 5:21). There it is: "the righteousness of God." When we are centered on the gospel, we see that all our longings for acceptance and significance are pointing us to the all-satisfying reality of being in Christ.

The problem is that we are all prone to drift away from the gospel, like a boat without an anchor. When we are not anchored in the truth of the gospel, we feel distant from God and unsure of his love for us. So we compensate by trying to earn his approval through our performance. Or we substitute the approval of people for God's approval. We perform for them.

Last week, we saw that one of the ways we "shrink the cross" is by pretending— minimizing our sin so we look better than we really are. We also limit the power of the gospel in our lives by performing—minimizing God's holiness so we can measure up.

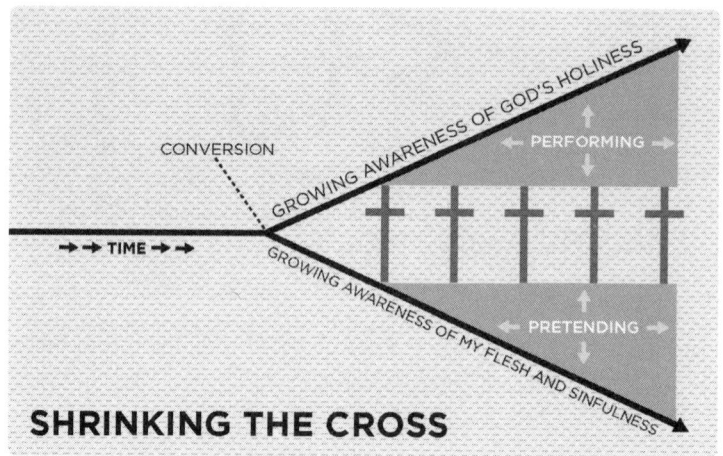

There are basically two kinds of righteousness (or right standing) in the Bible, "a righteousness of our own" and "the righteousness of God" (Philippians 3:9, Romans 10:3). Our righteousness is something we achieve through our performance. The righteousness of God is something we receive by faith. The difference between the two is the key to staying centered on the gospel, so let's see how the apostle Paul sorts this out.

Paul grew up in the school of religious elites. They tried to measure up by keeping the law of God. They couldn't, of course, so they made lots of laws that they could keep. That's what performing is all about—measuring yourself by what you can do. Paul and his friends were seeking to establish a righteousness of their own (Romans 10:3).

That's why performing minimizes God's holiness. Thinking we can impress God with our "right living" shows that we've reduced his standards far below what they actually are. Rather than being in awe of who God is, we convince ourselves that if we just try hard enough, we can earn God's love and approval.

Now, if anyone could be confident in his performance, it would have been Paul. He did everything right: "as to righteousness under the law, blameless" (Philippians 3:6). This was his spiritual report card, so to speak. But then he met Jesus, and it rocked his world. Everything that once made him feel acceptable was suddenly like a pile of trash compared to the righteousness of God. He had a choice: cling to his own righteousness or receive the righteousness of God in Christ. Report card or relationship? He chose the latter:

> *But whatever gain I had, I counted as loss for the sake of Christ. Indeed, I count everything as loss because of the surpassing worth of knowing Christ Jesus my Lord. For his sake I have suffered the loss of all things and count them as rubbish, in order that I may gain Christ and be found in him, not having a righteousness of my own that comes from the law, but that which comes through faith in Christ, the righteousness from God that depends on faith. (Philippians 3:7-9).*

The righteousness of God—the acceptance and approval we want most—is not something we earn through performance, but rather something we receive through faith. When we are not centered on the gospel, we will fall into a performance mentality again.

When we are performing, everything is about us. Everything we do and all our relationships are tainted by our need to prove ourselves. It makes us takers instead of givers. But when our right standing (righteousness) is grounded in Christ, then we are free to truly give. We can pursue excellence without being anxious; we can serve others without expecting anything in return; we can be ourselves without fear of rejection.

So we have a constant need to repent of sin and believe the gospel. To repent means to change our mind or think differently about something. In this case, we are thinking differently about our right standing, turning away from working on our own standing before God and others, and instead believing the promise that God is pleased with us because he is pleased with Jesus. When we embrace the gospel in this way, the infinite standard of God's holiness is no longer fearful or intimidating. It leads us to be thankful and love God even more because Jesus has met it for us. Our identity is in him. The good news of the gospel is not that God makes much of us, but that God frees us to make much of Jesus.

This is the everyday pattern of the Christian life: repentance and faith, repentance and faith, repentance and faith. As we walk this way, the gospel will take root more deeply in our souls, and Jesus and his cross will become bigger in the day-to-day reality of our lives.

SELF-ASSESSMENT:
ORPHANS VS. CHILDREN

This is a practical exercise to reveal our tendencies to base our identity on performance, and to take control of our lives. This exercise will help you identify all of the ways you try to depend on yourself and make yourself right. That will help you see all the ways you need to ask God for forgiveness and help. That's the first step in trusting Jesus for your right standing, and it will free you to serve Jesus and others. Read through each bulleted list. Under "The Orphan," check the box if you see that tendency in yourself. Underline the words that most apply. Under "The Son/Daughter," check the boxes that describe where you most want to grow, underlining the key words.

THE ORPHAN	THE SON / DAUGHTER
☐ Doesn't feel connected to God in daily life	☐ Feels connected to God throughout the day
☐ Anxious about friends, money, school, grades, etc.	☐ Feels freed from worry because of God's love for you
☐ Feels as if no one cares about you	☐ Feels forgiven and totally accepted
☐ Lives on a success/fail basis	☐ Trust in God's plan for your life
☐ Needs to look good	☐ Quick to pray about things
☐ Feels guilty and condemned	☐ Content in relationships b/c you are accepted by God
☐ Struggles to trust God with the future	☐ Is teachable by others
☐ Not very teachable	☐ Open to criticism b/c your identity is secure in Christ
☐ Is defensive when accused of error or weakness	☐ Able to takes risks—even to fail
☐ Needs to be right	☐ Encouraged by the Spirit working in you
☐ Lacks confidence	☐ Able to see God's goodness in dark times
☐ Solution to failure: "Try harder"	☐ Content with what you have
☐ Has a critical spirit (complaining and bitterness)	☐ Trusting less in self and more in the Holy Spirit
☐ Tears others down	☐ Is able to freely confess faults to others
☐ Tends to compare yourself with others	☐ Doesn't always have to be right
☐ Feels powerless to defeat the flesh	☐ Does not gain value from the praise of others
☐ Needs to be in control of situations and others	☐ Experiences more and more freedom from sin and bad habits
☐ Looks for satisfaction in "positions"	☐ Prayer is a vital, ongoing part of the day
☐ Looks for satisfaction in "possessions"	☐ Jesus is more and more the subject of conversation
☐ Tends to be motivated by obligation and duty, not love	☐ God truly satisfies your soul

lesson

LAW & GOSPEL

BIG IDEA

We are still thinking about how understanding the gospel impacts our lives, but now we are doing it by considering the gospel's relationship to the law. What is the law of God? Does God expect me to obey it? What is the purpose of the law? How does the law help me believe the gospel? How does the gospel help me obey the law? These are the questions before us in this lesson.

LESSON OVERVIEW

I. BIBLE CONVERSATION	Read and talk about the passage(s) [10 min]
II. ARTICLE	Read *The Law and the Gospel* together [10 min]
III. DISCUSSION	Process concepts together [15 min]
IV. EXERCISE	Apply the concepts using a specific exercise [20 min]
V. WRAP-UP	Final thoughts and prayer [5 min]

BIBLE CONVERSATION *10 minutes*

Romans 10:1–4 speaks of Christ being "the end of the law." The question you want your group to wrestle with is what does this mean? Does it mean God's law doesn't matter anymore? Hint: the answer is no, but if your group heads in that direction in the Bible conversation, you can let it slide because the article will bring the needed correction. The point of this Bible conversation is not to "solve the passage" but simply to get people thinking about

45

> the issue. So, if the questions only lead to more questions, that's good! The article will have plenty of answers.

SETUP   We have been talking about the gospel. One major dilemma or challenge in understanding the gospel centers on the role of the law—all the commands and expectations God places upon us. Let's start our conversation by reading and talking about a passage where Paul mentions this issue.

READ   Have someone read Romans 10:1–4 out loud.

ASK   What two types of righteousness seem to be contrasted in this passage?

ASK   What does this passage say about Jesus and his relationship to the law?

TRANSITION TO ARTICLE   This passage says that Christ is "the end of the law." But Jesus also said we're not to dismiss the law (Matthew 5:17–19). Which is it? What are we supposed to do with the law? Hopefully, this article will answer our questions along these lines. Let's read it together and then talk more about this.

ARTICLE *10 minutes*

Ask your group to turn to the article *The Law & The Gospel* in their Participant's Guide and read it aloud together, taking turns at the paragraph breaks.

TRANSITION TO DISCUSSION   We don't usually talk about "the law," at least not like people did in Paul's day. So let's talk about these concepts and see how they relate to our context.

DISCUSSION *15 minutes*

> *These questions are aimed at helping everyone understand the concepts in the article and connect them to their own beliefs and actions.*

ASK The author of the article talks about feeling like "you ought to be a better Christian." Where do you feel like you ought to be doing better right now?

ASK How does it feel to live under this sense of "ought" or "should"?

ASK Can you see how God's laws are all about love? Can you give some examples of how God's laws are meant to show us how to love others?

ASK Having read the article, how would you summarize the way the law and the gospel work together? How does the gospel relate to your sense of "ought" and "should"?

TRANSITION TO EXERCISE The Bible uses the phrase "under the law" to describe the experience of living our spiritual lives on the treadmill of what we "ought" to be or do. Here's the tension: If we try to live by the law, we are not living in light of the gospel. But if we dismiss the law altogether, we don't experience the gospel's power to help us obey the law. This tension affects the way we read the Bible so I want us to do an exercise to help us keep these things in their proper places as we read the Bible and follow Christ.

EXERCISE: The Gospel Grid & the Law
20 minutes

1. Turn to the Gospel Grid & the Law exercise with your group.

2. Read the explanation aloud. (Stop at the Practice section.)

3. Together, work through a few passages from the Practice section using the "gospel grid."

WRAP-UP *5 minutes*
Questions, comments, prayer.

lesson

ARTICLE 4
THE LAW & THE GOSPEL

Last week we talked about the concept of righteousness, which is our sense of being right with God. The gospel says that the only way we can be right with God is to be in Christ, who is our "wisdom from God, righteousness and sanctification and redemption" (1 Corinthians 1:30). When we struggle to believe the gospel, we are prone to pretend and perform. We pretend to be better than we are by minimizing our sin, and we minimize God's holiness by acting as if we could measure up to his holiness.

The idea that God accepts us in Christ, apart from our good or bad behavior, leads us to a very important question: What is the point of the law of God? Anyone who picks up the Bible can see that it is full of commands—things we are supposed to do and things we aren't supposed to do. Did you know that the whole law can be summed up like this: "You shall *love* the Lord your God with all your heart and with all your soul and with all your strength and with all your mind, and your neighbor as yourself" (Luke 10:27, emphasis added).

The law of God is not a just a bunch of rules. It's our guide to a life full of love, purpose, and meaning. The law of God shows us the path to true love. But love is not easy, especially when you consider the call to love God and everyone else with all of your strength!

So how can God's law of love and the gospel of God relate to each other? After all, if we are reconciled to God by grace and not by works, does it really matter whether or not we obey his command to love him and others?

If we don't understand the relationship between God's law and his gospel, we get off center in two ways. First, we can start to think God will love and accept us as long as we follow the rules. This is basing our sense of right standing and identity on how well we think we are keeping God's commands. When we do this we go back to trying to get our right standing on our own. This never works and becomes a huge burden where we are constantly working to get God's approval (with a sense of never measuring up) or we substitute the approval of people (with which we are never satisfied).

The other way we move away from the gospel is to think that it's okay if we don't keep God's commands. We might think something like "Nobody should judge what I do because God accepts us no matter what." This sounds like we are basing our righteousness in Christ, but it's actually finding our identity in breaking the rules and getting away with it! When we go this route, we are going back to a life of going our own way instead of God's way. This always brings brokenness into our lives and the mess of sin, sorrow, and death.

To avoid these pitfalls, we must understand the biblical relationship between law and gospel. In a nutshell, here's how God designed it to work: the law of love drives us to the gospel and the gospel frees us to love God and others (which is what obeying the law adds up to). An honest look at God and his commands shows us that we cannot measure up, and that drives us to Christ. Once we are united with Christ, the Holy Spirit gives us the desire and the power to love God and others.

How do we become the kind of people who love God and love others? Answer: through the gospel.

First, it is through the gospel that we become aware that we have broken God's law of love. Without the Spirit we would think all of our choices are fine. Did you know that feeling guilty when you do something wrong is one way you know that God is at work in your life? The first step of the gospel journey is to become aware that "all have sinned and fall short of the glory of God" (Romans 3:23), and that our disobedience to God's law places us under his curse (Galatians 3:10).

Second, it is through the gospel that we are freed from the curse of the law (Galatians 3:13–14). Through the life and death of Jesus, all who turn from their sins and come to Jesus in faith are both forgiven and made righteous. And by his resurrection, we are free to live for him (2 Corinthians 5:14–15). In biblical language, we are no longer "under law" (Romans 6:14).

Third, it is through the gospel that God gives us his Holy Spirit, who transforms our hearts and enables us to truly love God and others (Romans 5:5; John 17:26).

Thinking we can keep God's law and ignoring God's law are both self-centered. They are not concerned with loving God and wanting to love others, but with self: "I keep the rules" or "I break the rules." But the gospel frees us from our self-concern and turns us outward.

Romans 10:4 says, "Christ is the end of the law for righteousness to everyone who believes." In other words, the end, the goal, the point of the law is to drive us to Jesus. When we really "get" what this verse is saying, we begin to see that every command in Scripture points us in some way to Jesus, who fulfills that command for us and in us. He is our righteousness. We no longer need to establish our own.

When I became a Christian, I did all the right things (and mostly not the bad things), but I felt distant from God. So after a while I threw out the rules and did whatever I wanted, but that left me just as empty as before. Then it hit me: Christianity is not about keeping or not keeping the rules. It is about relationship with a person!

Imagine a teenager who lives on his own (we'll call him Max). Max had never had any parents or authorities, and therefore has never had any rules. He calls the shots in his life. One day Max met Sam, a teenager who grew up in a loving home. Max asked Sam what his life was like, so Sam told him about the rules and expectations in his home. Max felt sorry for Sam because he had all kinds of rules he had to follow. He couldn't understand how anyone could live like that.

Then he spent a weekend at Sam's house. He got there right before dinner. He and Max had to set the table, make the salad, and wash their hands before eating. It was slightly irritating for Max, who was getting hungry. When the whole family sat down around the table, Sam's dad started the meal with a blessing. As they passed the food around, his mom asked the kids about their day at school. While they ate, the kids told stories about the stuff that happened to them at school and practice. When someone chewed with his mouth open or got too silly, Sam's mom or dad would say something about it. Max was not used to that, but he also kind of liked it.

After dinner, they had to help clean up the dishes, which none of the kids really wanted to do, but those were the rules. Before bedtime, Sam's dad made sure all the kids had done their homework and were prepared for the next day. Max wasn't tired yet, but it was bedtime. Those were the rules. Dad read a story to the younger children, prayed for them all, and told them how much he loved them. Lights out.

On Monday Max went back to his life of freedom from the rules, but he had an ache in his heart. He missed being at Sam's house. The more he thought about it, the more he realized that the rules were more than rules. They were ways Sam's parents loved their family. It was their way of helping Sam live a life of joy and purpose. Sam didn't love all the rules, but what seemed to make everything work was how much his parents loved him, even when he failed. Their love empowered him to do things—even made him *want* to do things—that he would otherwise never do.

That's what hit me when I was going back and forth between trying to keep the law and not caring about the law. I had missed the point. I was reading the Bible, but not realizing that the Bible points me to a person—to Jesus! And when I stopped reading the Bible, I wasn't running away from a rule, but from a person. Suddenly I wanted to read the Bible to get to know Jesus. I wanted to sit around the table with him and his family, so to speak, and enjoy their friendship.

When I saw that the commands of God point me to Jesus, I became more concerned with obeying them, not to earn God's love, but because

I already had it. Every command in Scripture points us to our own inadequacy (the bottom line of the Cross Chart), magnifies the good and holy nature of God (the top line of the Cross Chart), and causes us to look to Jesus as the One who forgives our disobedience and enables our obedience. And that's how the law drives us to Jesus, and Jesus frees us to obey the law.

THE GOSPEL GRID & THE LAW

A "grid" is a pattern for thinking, a filter to run things through, a particular way of looking at something. Understanding the Bible and articulating the gospel in creative, relevant ways involves applying various grids to make sense of truth. In Lesson One we gave you what we call the "gospel grid," illustrated by the Cross Chart. This week we are going to learn how to understand the law of God through that grid.

Scripture is full of moral imperatives (commands) about loving God and others. Sometimes it is explicitly commanded. Sometimes it is implied. For instance, a verse may tell you not to lie. You can respond to this imperative in three different ways.

> LEGALISM: You know that it isn't loving people to lie. So you try your best not to lie. This is what it means to live under the law. You will inevitably discover that you cannot keep from lying, even when you lower your standards about what that means.
>
> LICENSE: You can admit from the start that you cannot obey this command and simply dismiss it as a biblical ideal you are not actually expected to obey. This is what it means to abuse God's grace and give in to sin.
>
> GOSPEL: This is the grid we want to learn. It goes like this:
>
>> 1. Loving people means speaking the truth to them. So God says, "Do not lie." (Top line of the Cross Chart: God's holiness)

2. I cannot obey this command on my own because I'm a sinner. (Bottom line of the Chart: my sinfulness)

3. Jesus did obey this perfectly. (I can point to countless examples in his earthly life as recorded in the Gospels.) Jesus did what I should do (but can't) as my substitute so that God can accept me (2 Corinthians 5:17).

4. Because Jesus obeyed the law perfectly and now lives in me, and because I am accepted by God, I am now free to obey this command by his grace and power at work in me.

Applying this grid to your study of the Bible will help you believe the gospel and obey the law without falling into legalism or license. This empowers you to experience the reality that the gospel changes everything.

PRACTICE

Read a passage together and apply this grid. (Pick from Philippians 4:4–7, James 2:1–7, 1 Peter 3:9)

What is the command? How does it express love for God and love for others?

Why can't you do it? (Be specific about your particular struggles to obey this command.)

How did Jesus do this perfectly? (Note specific examples in the Gospels.)

How can God's Spirit in you empower you to obey this command (in specific situations)?

lesson

LEADER'S GUIDE

REPENTANCE

BIG IDEA

This lesson deals with repentance. In our culture, this usually sounds like a bad thing—like getting called into the principal's office. Far from being bad or unusual, biblical repentance is the norm for gospel-centered living. Becoming more aware of God's holiness and our sinfulness leads us to repent and believe the gospel of Jesus. We are constantly turning from our performing and pretending so that we may live as sons and daughters. Biblical repentance frees us from our own ways of dealing with what we do wrong and makes a way for God's power to fill us and change us. So our aim in this lesson is to (1) expose the ways in which we practice false repentance and (2) move toward genuine repentance.

LESSON OVERVIEW

I. BIBLE CONVERSATION	Read and talk about the passage(s) [10 min]	
II. ARTICLE	Read *Lifestyle Repentance* together [10 min]	
III. DISCUSSION	Process concepts together [15 min]	
IV. EXERCISE	Apply the concepts using a specific exercise [20 min]	
V. WRAP-UP	Final thoughts and prayer [5 min]	

BIBLE CONVERSATION *10 minutes*

This text introduces the topic of repentance and will hopefully provoke some good questions. You do not need to figure everything out about this passage. Just allow it to get the conversation going.

INTRO QUESTION When the sins of others affect or bother you, what kinds of things do you need to see in them before you feel better about them or forgive them? *(I want them to feel bad about it, apologize, experience the consequences, turn from their sin so they can experience God's grace, etc.)*

TRANSITION We are usually a mixed bag of desires when it comes to people's sin. Sometimes we really want what is best for them. Sometimes we just want to feel better about ourselves. We're going to read a passage that shows Paul's desire for the Corinthians in this area.

READ Have someone read 2 Corinthians 7:5–13.

ASK What did Paul want from the Corinthians? *(Godly grief that leads to repentance.)*

ASK Why did he want this? *(For their good and progress in the faith.)*

ASK What was the fruit of repentance in their lives? (vv. 7, 11)

ASK How did their repentance affect Paul? *(He was comforted by God, not merely justified in his rebuke.)*

ARTICLE *10 minutes*

Ask your group to turn to the article *Lifestyle Repentance* in their Participant's Guide and read it aloud together, taking turns at the paragraph breaks.

DISCUSSION *15 minutes*

ASK What stood out most to you in this article?

ASK How would you explain the difference between true and false repentance in your own words?

ASK Do you see yourself tending more toward remorse or resolution?

ASK What do you think are some evidences or marks of true repentance?

TRANSITION TO EXERCISE For this to really take root in us, we have to talk about how we can practice genuine repentance in our lives. We are going to do an exercise that will help us identify counterfeit repentance and move us toward true repentance.

EXERCISE 20 minutes

This exercise will help your group identify forms of counterfeit repentance and practice genuine repentance—and we mean "practice" in a very literal sense. The group will process common responses of false repentance (and the underlying heart sins) in an effort to determine how people can truly repent in specific situations. You are practicing something that needs to be lived out in real life. Because repentance often carries a negative connotation, you will need to remind your group that it is good and normal. This exercise is an expression of a loving community.

1. Turn to the Practicing Repentance exercise with your group.

2. Read through the instructions given and work through the exercise with your group.

WRAP-UP 5 minutes

Questions, comments, prayer.

lesson 5
ARTICLE 5: LIFESTYLE REPENTANCE

People often talk about repenting and believing in the past tense, something they did when they became a Christian. In that sense the gospel is viewed as a ticket to an afterlife with God, like a reservation for a table in heaven when the time comes. But does that sound like what Jesus had in mind when he announced his ministry in Mark 1? When Jesus began his ministry on earth, his main message was, "the kingdom of God is at hand; repent and believe in the gospel" (Mark 1:15).

Jesus was making an announcement that God was breaking into our world. Through Christ, God was speaking and working in the context of our daily lives, and giving us access to his presence and power like never before. In light of this reality—the kingdom of God at hand—Jesus said we should rethink how we are living our lives. That's what it means to repent—to reconsider how we are living life since we now have the option to live life with God.

The kingdom of God includes heaven, but it is also right here, right now. Our new life with God begins when we believe the good news about Jesus, the Son of God, and it grows in us and through us as we keep believing and applying that news to every area of our lives.

Here's a simple analogy. Let's say that in order to have a good relationship with your parents you have to believe they love you and that obeying them is in your best interest (crazy, I know). It would be ridiculous to say that you only have to believe that once. Nobody ever says, "My parents are totally unreasonable and have no idea what I am going through, but when I was nine I believed they loved me and knew what was best for me so it's all good; we have a great relationship!"

In the same way, we believe the gospel to begin a relationship with God, and we continue believing it to grow in our relationship with God. Jesus saves us and changes us. To use theological terms, Jesus makes us right with God (justification) and frees us to obey God (sanctification). We never stop needing the gospel.

The problem, as we have seen, is that we struggle to stay God-centered. No matter how much we grow in our faith, we still have a tendency to pretend and perform. That's why Jesus gives us these two steps: repent and believe. We constantly have to rethink how we are living in light of the gospel.

For example, when we find ourselves harboring bitterness toward someone, we have to rethink it: God did not store up his anger against us, but poured it out on Jesus in my place. Therefore, we are free to forgive others as we have been forgiven in Christ. That is life in the kingdom! Or when we are anxious about something, we have to reconsider where our security lies: our well-being is not tied up in our achievements or the approval of others. In Christ, God has become our loving Father, and he knows what we need. I am free to rest in his provision and approval. Because the kingdom of God routinely comes into conflict with "normal life," we never stop needing to repent and believe.

For most of us, the word *repentance* has a negative connotation. We only repent when we do something *really* bad, or when we get caught. We usually think we should feel really sorry about what we've done, maybe beat ourselves up over it, and then do something to make up for it. In other words, repentance often becomes more about *us* than about God or the people we've sinned against. We want to feel better. We want things to be back to normal. We want to know that we've done our part, so that our guilt is eased and we can move on with life. Whenever our repentance is about us, it's probably not about life in the kingdom.

We can identify this kind of false repentance by looking for patterns of *remorse* and *resolution* in our dealings with sin. Remorse: "I can't believe I did that!" Resolution: "I promise to do better next time."

Remorse and resolution point to two great misunderstandings about our hearts. First, we think too highly of ourselves. We do not truly believe the depth of our sin and brokenness (the bottom line of the Cross Chart). This leads us to react in surprise when sin manifests itself: "I can't believe I just did that!" In other words, "That's not what I'm *really* like!" Second, we think we have the power to change ourselves. We think that if we make resolutions or try harder next time, we'll be able to fix the problem. Think about the last time you did something wrong and had to face it. Did you respond with remorse and/or resolution?

These patterns taint our attitudes toward others as well. Because we think so highly of ourselves, we respond to others' sin with harshness and disapproval. We are very lenient toward our own sin, but we resent theirs! And because we think we can change ourselves, we are frustrated when other people aren't changing *themselves* faster. We become judgmental, impatient, and critical.

The gospel calls us to (and empowers us for) **true repentance**. According to the Bible, true repentance

> IS ORIENTED TOWARD GOD, NOT ME. Psalm 51:4: "Against *you, you only*, have I sinned and done what is evil in your sight. . . . " Repentance eventually moves toward people, but it begins with humility before God.

> IS MOTIVATED BY TRUE GODLY SORROW AND NOT JUST SELFISH REGRET. 2 Corinthians 7:10: "For godly grief produces a repentance that leads to salvation without regret, whereas worldly sorrow produces death." Worldly sorrow is what you feel when you get caught, or don't like the consequences, or feel bad that someone else was hurt. So if you say, "I'm sorry if you were hurt by what I did," that is not true repentance.

IS CONCERNED WITH THE HEART, NOT JUST WITH EXTERNAL ACTIONS. Psalm 51:10: "Create in me a clean heart, O God, and renew a right spirit within me." A repentant person wants to do the right thing in the right way, for the right reasons.

LOOKS TO JESUS FOR DELIVERANCE FROM THE PENALTY AND POWER OF SIN. Acts 3:19–20: "Repent, therefore, and turn again, that your sins may be blotted out, that times of refreshing may come from the presence of the Lord, and that he may send the Christ appointed for you, Jesus." Often the lightening of consequences, the passing of hardship, or the graciousness of others too quickly relieves us. True repentance turns to Jesus for ultimate healing and comfort.

Instead of excusing our sin or falling into patterns of remorse and resolution, true repentance leads us to confess and receive.

- Confess: "I *did* do that." ("That IS what I'm really like!")
- Receive: "Lord, forgive me! You are my only hope."

As we learn to live in light of the gospel, this kind of true repentance should become normal for us. We will stop being surprised by our sin, so we will be able to more honestly admit it. And we will stop believing we can fix ourselves so we will more quickly turn to Jesus for forgiveness and transformation.

Sin is a condition, not just a behavior, so true repentance is a lifestyle, not just an occasional practice. Repentance is not something we do only once (when we are converted), or only periodically (when we feel *really* guilty). Repentance is ongoing, and conviction of sin is a mark of God's fatherly love for us. "Those whom I love, I reprove and discipline, so be zealous and repent" (Revelation 3:19).

So what are you repenting of?

lesson

EXERCISE

5 PRACTICING REPENTANCE

We often make excuses for our sin to avoid the hard work of repentance. Below is a list of some common excuses—and (in parentheses) the inner thoughts they reveal. Take a minute to look over the list and then use the questions below to help each other practice genuine repentance.

- **I was just being honest.** (Can't you handle the truth?)
- **I'm just saying what I feel.** (There's nothing wrong with sharing my feelings.)
- **I was only kidding.** (I can say something hurtful if I act like it was a joke.)
- **I misunderstood you.** (I don't want you to know that I was really judging you.)
- **You misunderstood me.** (I'm not as bad as you think.)
- **That's just who I am.** (I can't help my personality, so that excuses my behavior.)
- **I made a mistake.** (It was minor and don't we all make mistakes?)
- **I didn't mean to do it.** (I didn't mean to get caught.)
- **I'm having a bad day.** (I deserve a pass for anything hurtful I did.)
- **What I did wasn't as bad as _____.** (I didn't do something as bad as my friends, so it's not that big of a deal.)

Which of the excuses listed above can you identify with?

What is a recent example (or a typical situation) when you used one of these excuses instead of truly being broken and repentant over your sin?

As a group, describe what true repentance would look like in these cases (using real examples shared in the group), following the steps below.

> STEP 1: Acknowledge that you have sinned against God.
>
> STEP 2: Confess forms of remorse and resolution.
>
> STEP 3: Identify and confess the underlying heart motivations that drive you to this sin ("the sin beneath the sin").
>
> STEP 4: Receive God's forgiveness by faith.
>
> STEP 5: Rely upon God's power to turn away from sin.

Repeat this process, working through as many responses as time allows: identify excuses, share examples, and practice true repentance.

HEART IDOLATRY

BIG IDEA

We've said that the Christian walk consists of two repeated steps: repentance and faith. In Lesson Five, we dealt with repentance. Now we turn our attention to the topic of faith. Remember, we grow by trusting Jesus and believing the gospel. That's the emphasis of this week's discussion and exercise. Easy enough, right? This week's goal is to take "believing the gospel" out of the abstract and make it concrete.

LESSON OVERVIEW

I. BIBLE CONVERSATION	Read and talk about the passage(s) [10 min]	
II. ARTICLE	Read *Heart Idolatry* together [10 min]	
III. DISCUSSION	Process concepts together [30 min]	
IV. WRAP-UP	Final thoughts and prayer [5 min]	

BIBLE CONVERSATION *10 minutes*

READ Have someone read Mark 1:15.

SAY If Jesus had a bumper sticker (which he would not have!), it would say, "Repent and believe, for the kingdom of heaven is at hand." This was his tagline and the main subject of his teaching.

ASK What do you think Jesus meant when he said, "Repent and believe?"

ASK What kind of response was he looking for?

ASK According to this verse, what exactly are we to believe?

TRANSITION TO ARTICLE The article we're about to read focuses on what it means to believe the gospel and how that produces growth in our lives. Let's read it together.

ARTICLE 10 minutes

Ask your group to turn to the article *Heart Idolatry* in their Participant's Guide and read it aloud together, taking turns at the paragraph breaks.

TRANSITION TO DISCUSSION Let's talk about the concept of heart idols, and especially our heart idols.

DISCUSSION 30 minutes

ASK First of all, does everyone understand the concept of heart idols?

If people seem unsure, go back and read that section of the article again.

ASK Using the list in the article, which one or two would you say are your biggest heart idols?

Have everyone share.

ASK How does this idol manifest itself in your life? In other words, what surface sins can you see in your life that are connected to a deeper idol?

SAY The way to deal with heart idols is to apply the gospel to our specific issues. Let's talk about how we can apply the gospel to our heart idols.

Walk through the following questions with different people in the group, applying the gospel communally to the various heart idols that have been identified.

ASK How do you see your heart idols failing you? To put it another way, what does it promise you, but in the end does not deliver?

ASK How does the gospel "deliver" in this area? *(How does it actually satisfy your desires or meet your needs more fully than your idols?)*

ASK What do you need to receive by faith from the gospel in order to defeat the power of these idols in your life? In other words, what specific biblical truths do you need to "really believe" to combat the idolatries of your heart? Do you find it difficult to believe these truths? Why?

ASK How do your heart idols undermine your ability to love?

ASK How does the gospel free you to love others well?

WRAP-UP *5 minutes*

Questions, comments, prayer.

In your prayer time, focus on "praying the gospel into each other"—that is, praying specifically that the truths of the gospel would defeat the power of the unique idols in each person's life.

lesson

6 HEART IDOLATRY
ARTICLE

Pop quiz: What one thing should we do to grow more in our relationship with God?

A number of things come to mind: read the Bible, pray, find Christian friends, repent of sin, and more. The crowds brought this exact question to Jesus in John 6. His answer may surprise you: "Then they said to him, 'What must we do, to be doing the works of God?' Jesus answered them, 'This is the work of God, that you believe in him whom he has sent'" (John 6:28–29).

Notice that they are asking Jesus what they must do to live a life that pleases God. Jesus answers that the *work* of God is to *believe*. Was that your answer on the pop quiz?

We tend to think that being a Christian is about doing good things and not doing bad things. But there is always more to the story than what we do and say. They are really just symptoms of what is going on in our hearts—what we believe. Think of it like a physical sickness. Any good doctor knows that the symptoms are not the real problem. They are signs that point to the sickness inside us. A doctor can treat the symptoms to make us feel better, but true healing means getting to the root problems.

To see how this works, take a minute to discuss this question: Why do we lie?

The easy answer is to say that we lie because we are sinners, but the easy answer is usually not the most helpful one. Every time we lie (behavior), there is more to the story (belief). We lie because, in the moment, there is something we want more or love more than the truth. If we lie to impress, then we want people's approval more than God's. If we lie to avoid consequences, then we love our comfort more than genuine relationship.

This is why the most important thing we can do is to believe. What we believe (want, love, trust) is the root of what we do. Getting this right is crucial to growing in our relationship with God. Every one of our struggles has symptoms that point to a deeper problem. We call the symptoms "surface sins," and the sickness "heart idolatry."

An idol is an image or object that represents a god. For example, when Moses was on the mountain getting the Ten Commandments from God, the people were restless without their leader. So they made a golden statue of a calf and worshipped it. Idols are false gods that take the place of the one, true God. You are probably not going to make a statue of a baby cow, but there are things in your heart that take the place of God. Any time our behavior is a result of wanting or loving something more than God, we are worshipping that "idol" instead of God. Behavior is the symptom. Heart idolatry is the sickness.

Underneath every external sin is a heart idol—a false god that has eclipsed the true God in our thoughts or desires. The key to gospel-driven transformation is learning to repent of the "sin beneath the sin"—the deeply rooted idolatry and unbelief that drive our more visible sins.

As a case study, let's take the surface sin of gossip—talking about people behind their backs in judgmental or destructive ways. Why do we gossip? What are we looking for that we should find in God? Here are some common heart idols that can manifest themselves in the surface sin of gossip:

- **The idol of approval** (I want the approval of the people I'm talking to.)
- **The idol of control** (I'm using gossip as a way to manipulate/control others.)
- **The idol of reputation** (I want to feel important, so I cut someone else down verbally.)

- **The idol of success** (Someone is succeeding—and I'm not—so I gossip about him.)
- **The idol of security** (Talking about others masks my own insecurity.)
- **The idol of pleasure** (Someone else is enjoying life—and I'm not—so I attack her.)
- **The idol of knowledge** (Talking about people is a way of showing I know more.)
- **The idol of recognition** (Talking about others gets people to notice me.)
- **The idol of respect** (That person disrespected me, so I'm going to disrespect him.)

All these idols are false gods promoting false gospels. Every one of these things—approval, control, reputation, success, security, pleasure, knowledge, recognition, and respect—is something we already have in Jesus because of the gospel! But when we do not remember and believe the gospel, we turn to these idols to give us what only Jesus can truly give us.

Another way to identify your particular heart idols is to ask: *What do I love, trust, or fear?* For example, if I fear being rejected or isolated socially, associating with the in-crowd will probably be my idol (because it promises to deliver me from the "hell" of unpopularity). If I trust "having enough," security will probably be my idol (because it promises that I'll never be without anything). If I love order and structure, control will probably be my idol (because if I'm in charge, I can make sure things are in order).

Reflecting on the "sin beneath our sin" shows why the gospel is essential for true heart change. It's possible to repent of surface sins for a lifetime and yet never address the deeper heart issues behind them! At the moment I sin, an idol has taken God's place in my soul. I am trusting in that idol, rather than in God, to be my Savior. I need to apply the gospel by (1) *repenting* of my deep heart idolatry and (2) *believing*—that is, turning my mind toward the specific gospel promises that break the power of the idols that are most typically a struggle for me.

Let's go back again to our example of gossip. Let's imagine that I have identified *respect* as the dominant idol that drives me to gossip. After I acknowledge my sin and repent of it, I exercise faith in two ways. First, I pause and worship Jesus because he laid aside his right to be respected, becoming humbled to the point of death (Philippians 2:5–11). Second, I remind myself of the gospel truth that I no longer need to crave the respect of others because I have the approval of God through faith in Jesus (2 Corinthians 5:17–21). Whether people respect me or not is not important: God's grace has freed me from demanding my own respect, and now I live for the fame and honor of Jesus (1 Corinthians 10:31, John 5:44).

It's like getting suds out of a milk jug. If you put a little water in the jug, swirl it around, and then pour it out, you will still have suds. This is what we usually do to deal with our sin. We add a little prayer or church to our life and swish it around, but in the end we don't change that much. The only way to get rid of suds in a milk jug is to let the jug sit under the water until it fills and overflows. The expulsive power of the water flushes out the suds. If you want to uproot the idols in your life and be cleansed of your sin, you have to sit under the love of God toward you in Christ, so that the Spirit can make Jesus real to you. When that happens, the beauty and truth and power of the gospel fills you up, and flushes out the sins beneath the sins.

This is what God promises to do when we come to him in faith: "'If anyone thirsts, let him come to me and drink. Whoever believes in me . . . Out of his heart will flow rivers of living water'" (John 7:37-38). Go to Jesus in repentance and faith. Ask him to come into your life and fill you with himself. This is a prayer he always answers *yes*. Then every time you notice that you have turned from him toward an idol, go back, keep repenting, keep believing in the forgiveness of sins, keep asking for his Spirit to fill you and change you. That's the life of faith. That's how the kingdom of God comes into our lives.

MISSION

lesson **7** LEADER'S GUIDE

BIG IDEA

The gospel is simultaneously at work in us and through us. Inwardly, our desires and motives are being changed as we repent and believe the gospel. As we experience Christ's love in this way, we are compelled to go to those around us and share God's love with them. God's grace brings renewal everywhere, in us and through us.

LESSON OVERVIEW

I. BIBLE CONVERSATION	Read and talk about the passage(s) [10 min]	
II. ARTICLE	Read *The Gospel Propels Us Outward* together [10 min]	
III. DISCUSSION	Process concepts together [15 min]	
IV. EXERCISE	Apply the concepts using a specific exercise [20 min]	
V. WRAP-UP	Final thoughts and prayer [5 min]	

BIBLE CONVERSATION *10 minutes*

Galatians 5:13–15 establishes the biblical foundation for this lesson's major concept. The challenge, as it has been all along, is to get past what we believe "on paper" and see how we fail to live out that belief in real life. You won't get there in a short discussion of these verses, but, coupled with the article and exercise, this passage serves as a good "mirror" by which we can see our actual lives.

READ Galatians 5:13–15 aloud two or three times.

ASK How is it possible to use our freedom as an opportunity to sin? What are some things that keep us from serving one another as this passage instructs?

TRANSITION TO ARTICLE What does all this have to do with the gospel or gospel-centered living? Our tendency is to think of transformation as a personal, inward reality. It is that, but it is also an outward, expressed reality. This article will explain that in more depth.

ARTICLE *10 minutes*

Ask your group to turn to the article *The Gospel Propels Us Outward* in their Participant's Guide and read it aloud together, taking turns at the paragraph breaks.

TRANSITION TO DISCUSSION We are going to be working with this diagram for the next few lessons, so let's spend some time talking about these concepts.

DISCUSSION *15 minutes*

ASK How many of you feel like the Christian life—especially mission—is more like something we are supposed to do than something we get to do? Why do you think it feels that way sometimes?

ASK How do you want to "live out" your faith more?

ASK What are some practical ways you can "invite in"?

TRANSITION TO EXERCISE Okay, let's see if we can relate this to our actual lives. We are going to look at a series of questions that I want you to answer in the context of your life. Feel free to ask questions of the group if you get stuck. We can help each other work through this if we need to. The most important thing in these exercises is to be honest with yourself.

LEADER'S GUIDE

EXERCISE 20 minutes

Turn to the exercise Getting to the Heart of Mission.

> *Note:* "Mission" is broadly defined here as anything that blesses the world around us in word or deed.
>
> Give people enough time to answer the questions on their own. After people have completed the exercise, use these questions to encourage some sharing:

ASK How many of your situations involve a co-worker? Classmate? Family member? Friend? Other? *(This will give everyone a chance to share without having to say a whole lot. It will also give you an idea of how many people were able to identify something.)*

ASK for a volunteer (or pick one). Take the person's situation and have the group work through it by applying the gospel to the person's barriers. Ask the group how the gospel addresses the emotional, physical, intellectual, and spiritual barriers to mission in this person's situation? *(Repeat with other situations as you have time.)*

TRANSITION TO WRAP-UP This has been really good. It helps us to see mission not as an obligation, but as a natural outworking of the gospel.

I can address my lack of mission not by addressing mission, but by addressing my unbelief in the gospel. In the next couple of lessons we will apply this concept to conflict and forgiveness.

WRAP-UP 5 minutes

Questions, comments, prayer.

> **DON'T FORGET:** I'm going to ask you to complete a short exercise before you come next time. It is listed in Lesson 8, under Getting to the Heart of Forgiveness.

lesson

ARTICLE 7

THE GOSPEL PROPELS US OUTWARD

What do people at your school think about Christianity, or Christians?

Would people say that being a Christian is no fun, outdated, weird, judgmental, or fine if that's what works for you? You probably hear these kinds of opinions all the time. As we learn to live a gospel-centered life, we become increasingly aware that many people around us are centered on other things. Some people mock God, while others have just never thought much about God. In either case, it often makes us feel like keeping our faith to ourselves.

What kinds of people or situations are challenging for you when it comes to living a gospel-centered life?

Much of what we have talked about in this study has been focused on what the gospel is and how it changes us. But now we are following the movement of the gospel as it flows through us into the lives of people around us.

The grace of God is always going somewhere—moving forward, extending God's kingdom, and propelling his people toward love and service to others. This is the mission of God: to bless the world with the gospel through our words and deeds. That is, God works through us both to tell people about the gospel and to show them the gospel by how we speak and act. As we learn to live in light of the gospel, we will increasingly feel the gospel moving us outward.

The chart below reminds us that God's grace has both an inward and an outward movement that mirror each other. Internally, the grace of God helps me see my sin, respond in repentance and faith, and then experience the joy that comes when God works in me. Externally, the grace of God moves me to see opportunities for love and service, respond in repentance and faith, and experience joy that comes when God works through us.

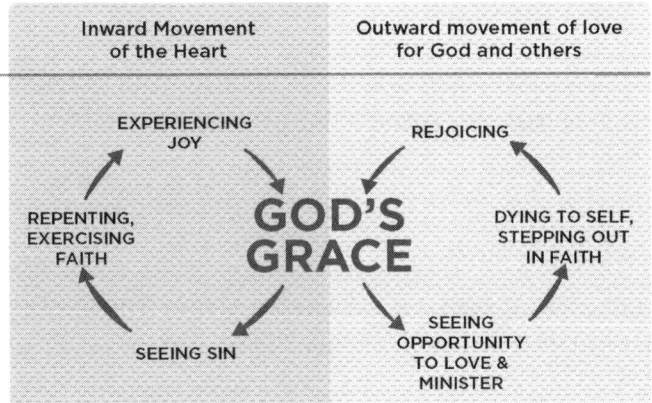

What does this outward movement of the gospel look like in real life? There are probably a thousand expressions of mission, but we can capture the heart of it with the simple rhythm of "living out" and "inviting in."

Living out the gospel means we apply the truth of the gospel to every area of our life. Our faith is not just something we do at church or youth group. It's who we are—"in Christ"—and therefore affects what we do everywhere. We do not isolate ourselves from the world; instead we want to move into the world and share God's love in any way we can. Here are some specific ways you can live out the gospel:

- Encourage those around you.
- Withhold gossip, sarcasm, and slander.
- Gently correct what is not good.
- Stand up for what is good.

- Tell people about Jesus (explain the gospel, share your own story, talk about how the gospel applies to situations they are facing, etc.).
- Help others in practical ways, even when it's not fun or costs you money.
- Listen well, especially to the concerns and questions people have.
- Choose to do the right thing, even when there is pressure to do otherwise.

Jesus took on a human body to show us what life with God is like. What he said and did show us what God is like and what he does. By living out our faith in the normal stuff of our lives, we show people what a life centered on the gospel looks like. But we do more than show people. We also invite them in so they can see for themselves.

Jesus welcomed anyone who was interested in learning from him. He regularly shared meals, conversations, and life with others, inviting them to encounter the kingdom of God. In the same way, we invite others to hang out with us so they can see and experience the gospel with us. We're not trying to get people to just come to church or youth group. We're looking to *be the church* among them. Here are some specific ways we invite people in:

- Ask questions that lead to meaningful conversation.
- Invite people to come with you to lunch, a party, church, a youth group event—really just whatever you are doing.
- Introduce people to your friends (don't be protective or jealous).
- Be honest about your struggles; it helps people open up about theirs.
- Initiate conversation with people who are different from you.
- Don't hide your faith.

Think about the people around you: who needs encouragement, prayer, friendship, and help? How could you move toward these people as God has moved toward you in Christ?

The more we experience the gospel personally, the more compelled we are to make our faith public. Mission is not just something we "should do." It is a natural overflow of the gospel's work inside us. If you aren't motivated to love, serve, and speak the gospel to people, the answer isn't to "just do it." The answer is to consider what might be short-circuiting the outward movement of grace in your life: fear, pride, selfishness, lack of repentance, disconnectedness from God's people, etc. Bring these things before God and ask him to renew your heart. A changed heart is the fuel for mission.

lesson

EXERCISE 7

GETTING TO THE HEART OF MISSION

EXAMINING YOUR HEART FOR MISSION

1. What opportunities do you have to help or care for someone, in which you are not motivated to do what you "should"? *(Here are some categories to jump-start your thinking: encouraging or praying for someone; sharing the gospel with someone; helping someone in need; taking a stand for something good.)*

2. What heart issues hinder you from doing these things? As you pray and reflect on the root of your inaction, what is God showing you about yourself? Be as specific and thorough as you can about the things that keep you from expressing gospel-centered love toward others. *(Some examples of common root issues include fear of rejection, insecurity, lack of love, selfishness with time, and feelings of inadequacy.)*

3. Repentance: What sin do you see in yourself that you need to repent of? How will you move toward these people?

4. Faith: What specific gospel promises or truths are you not really believing? How will you trust God to help or change you as you reach out to others?

FORGIVENESS

lesson
LEADER'S GUIDE

BIG IDEA

The gospel that works in us always works through us. It shows its power in our relationships and actions. One key way this happens is when we forgive others biblically.

LESSON OVERVIEW

I. BIBLE CONVERSATION	Read and talk about the passage(s) [10 min]	
II. ARTICLE	Read *The Gospel Empowers Us to Forgive* together [10 min]	
III. EXERCISE	Apply the concepts using a specific exercise [40 min]	
IV. WRAP-UP	Final thoughts and prayer [5 min]	

BIBLE CONVERSATION *10 minutes*

> *The point in this passage is pretty straightforward. But, of course, simple does not equal easy.*

SETUP The passage we are going to read is pretty straightforward. It's one of Jesus's parables. So as we read, look for the point of the story.

READ Matthew 18:21–35 out loud.

ASK Okay, what is the point of the story?

83

> **ASK** If you had to explain what it means to forgive someone, what would you say?

> **TRANSITION TO ARTICLE** Forgiveness isn't easy. This article will explain biblical forgiveness, and then we'll get into the homework from last week.

ARTICLE *10 minutes*

Ask your group to turn to the article *The Gospel Empowers Us to Forgive* in their Participant's Guide and read it aloud together, taking turns at the paragraph breaks.

> **ASK** Based on the article, what seem to be the important aspects of forgiveness?

> **TRANSITION TO EXERCISE** Okay, let's get to the hard part: how do we do at forgiving others?

EXERCISE *40 minutes*

You gave the first half of this exercise—Getting to the Heart of Forgiveness—to your group last week, and they should have answered the questions on their own.

> **ASK** What did you guys think of the homework? Was it hard to do, insightful, convicting, etc.? Why?

> **ASK** someone to share his or her answer to question 2, and then do the same for questions 3–6. *(You want people to share some of what they wrote down, but they don't need to share all of their answers, and they definitely don't need to use people's names.)*

APPLICATION QUESTIONS

This is the second part of the exercise, which you will do as a group. Taking some of the situations that have been shared, the group will talk about how the gospel can empower us to forgive in those situations. This applies the truths you've been talking about for weeks to this important issue. Here are the questions.

1. **Explain** how understanding the gospel can enable you to have compassion and genuine love toward people you need to forgive. (Be specific to your situations.)

2. **Describe** some of the specific steps of love you will take in these relationships. This is not theory! We are, as a group, helping each other to live out the gospel. We will provide accountability toward that goal.

TRANSITION TO WRAP-UP   It's hard to do this stuff, but this is what "faith working through love" is all about. Let's take some time to pray for one another as we pursue the people we need to love and forgive this week.

WRAP-UP *5 minutes*
Questions, comments, prayer.

lesson

ARTICLE 8
THE GOSPEL EMPOWERS US TO FORGIVE

Forgiving people who hurt us is one of the most difficult things to do in life. And the deeper the pain, the more challenging it gets. We often feel confused about what real forgiveness looks like. Are we to "forgive and forget"? Is that even possible? And what exactly does it mean to "love my enemy"? What about the person who sexually abused me? Or the friend who spread rumors about me? Or my sibling who says he or she is sorry but keeps doing the same thing over and over? Or the teacher who obviously doesn't like me?

We have seen that when, through the work of the Spirit, the gospel really takes root *in* us, the truths of the gospel begins to work out *through* us. Forgiveness is one area where the gospel must "go to work" in our lives. In fact, forgiving others really isn't possible unless we are living in light of God's forgiveness ourselves. So let's consider how the gospel moves us toward forgiveness.

The gospel begins with God's movement toward us. God takes the initiative, though he is the offended party. He acted to reconcile the relationship "while we were God's enemies" (Romans 5:10). Our sin had separated us from him (Isaiah 59:2). He had every right to condemn us, to resist us, and to sever the relationship, but he did not. Instead, he moved toward us: "While we were still sinners, Christ died for us" (Romans 5:8).

However, reconciliation with God requires our repentance. By forgiving our sin, God extends the *offer* of reconciliation, but reconciliation is not complete until we repent and receive his forgiveness by faith. Notice how both dynamics are reflected in 2 Corinthians 5:19–20: "In Christ God was reconciling the world to himself, not counting their trespasses against them, and entrusting to us the message of reconciliation. Therefore, we are ambassadors for Christ, God making his appeal through us. We implore you on behalf of Christ, be reconciled to God." God initiates and offers forgiveness, but our response of repentance and faith is essential.

So we might summarize God's forgiveness this way: By moving toward us, God invites and enables us to move toward him. The gospel starts with God (the offended party) moving toward us (the offenders). He cancels our debt and opens to us an opportunity for reconciliation. If we acknowledge our sin and repent, we are reconciled to God and able to enjoy our relationship with him.

What, then, does it look like for us to forgive others as God has forgiven us? This, after all, is what God commands: "Be kind to one another, tenderhearted, forgiving one another, as God in Christ forgave you" (Ephesians 4:32). Scripture assumes that if we have truly experienced God's forgiveness in the gospel, we will be radically forgiving toward others. By contrast, if we are unforgiving, resentful, or bitter toward others, it is a sure sign that we are not living out of the deep joy and freedom of the gospel.

Our forgiveness of others is intended to mirror the forgiveness God has given us. We are to take the initiative: "If you are offering your gift at the altar and there remember that your brother has something against you, leave your gift there before the altar and go. First be reconciled to your brother, and then come and offer your gift" (Matthew 5:23–24). We are to offer forgiveness and open a door for reconciliation.

But reconciliation is only possible when the other person repents. Christian author and counselor Dan Allender has suggested a helpful analogy: "Forgiveness involves a heart that cancels the debt but does not lend new money until repentance occurs."[1] Like God, we take the

---

1. Dr. Dan B. Allender and Dr. Tremper Longman III, *Bold Love* (Colorado Springs: NavPress, 1992), p.162.

initiative to move toward those who have offended us, and we invite them to move toward us in repentance.

What this means is that our work is not done once we have forgiven someone. Our heart's desire is not simply to forgive the offense, but ultimately to see the other person reconciled to God and to us. We cannot make this happen, but we are to pray for it, long for it, and welcome it. Where do we find the power to do this? After all, it's hard enough just *forgiving* someone who has hurt us. How do we find the grace and strength to pursue reconciliation?

The answer, of course, is the gospel. The gospel doesn't just show us *how* to forgive; it *empowers* us to forgive.

Often our awareness of our own sin is very small, while our awareness of another's sin is very large. Our underlying feeling is that *we* deserve to be forgiven, but the person who offended us does not. When we think like that we are living with a small view of God's holiness, a small view of our own sin, and a small view of the cross of Jesus.

As we grow in our awareness of God's holiness and our sin, we see how much we need forgiveness also. We also don't deserve to be forgiven; yet God forgives us in Christ. On that basis we also forgive those who have sinned against us (Matthew 6:14-15; Ephesians 4:32). Remember how much your forgiveness cost Jesus. Think about him on the cross, naked, nailed, suffering, and calling out to God, "Father, forgive them, for they know not what they do" (Luke 23:34). Ask for the Spirit to help you see the people who have wronged you with the same compassion that Jesus has extended to you.

This forgiveness *is* costly. It means canceling a debt when we feel we have every right to demand payment. It means absorbing the pain, hurt, shame, and grief of someone's sin against us. It means longing for repentance and restoration. But this is exactly how God has acted toward us in Jesus Christ. And through the gospel, the Holy Spirit empowers us to do the same toward others.

lesson
EXERCISE 8

GETTING TO THE HEART OF FORGIVENESS

HOMEWORK

(Answer these questions before your meeting. You may need a separate sheet of paper.)

1. Think of one or two people you need to forgive (or forgive more deeply). If you have a hard time thinking of someone, ask God to reveal someone to you.

Here are some scenarios and feelings that might bring someone to mind: someone you have distanced yourself from; people you feel uncomfortable around; people you no longer enjoy; arguments or conflicts you keep rehearsing in your mind; someone who said or did something that hurt you; feelings of anger, bitterness, irritation, fear, gossip, or a critical spirit. *(Write down one or two people who come to mind.)*

2. What irritates or disturbs you most about this person?

3. What issues of "justice" are involved in the situation? How has this person wronged you, hurt you, or sinned against you?

4. What conditions do you instinctively want to place on this person before you truly forgive him or her? In others words, what does your heart want to require from this person before you forgive him or her?

What specifically would you desire the person to say or do?

5. Describe your own debt before God. How has God, in Christ, cancelled and forgiven your debt? Do not rush through this question. Take time to describe your indebtedness in terms of the specific ways sin manifests itself in your life.

6. How has your previous way of relating to these people reflected a small view of your own debt and a small view of Christ's forgiveness?

CONFLICT

lesson 9 **LEADER'S GUIDE**

BIG IDEA

Conflict is something we all experience regularly, but often handle very badly. The gospel gives us a pattern and a means to healthy conflict resolution.

LESSON OVERVIEW

I. BIBLE CONVERSATION	Read and talk about the passage(s) [10 min]	
II. ARTICLE	Read *The Gospel Helps Us Fight Fairly* together [10 min]	
III. DISCUSSION	Process concepts together [10 min]	
IV. EXERCISE	Apply the concepts using a specific exercise [30 min]	
V. WRAP-UP	Final thoughts and prayer [5 min]	

BIBLE CONVERSATION *10 minutes*

READ Romans 12:14-21

ASK What are all the ways you see in these verses that we should deal with conflict?

ASK What do you think it means to "be overcome by evil"?

ASK What do you think it means to "overcome evil with good"?

> **TRANSITION TO ARTICLE**   This article will take us deeper into how (and how not) to handle conflict in our relationships.

ARTICLE *10 minutes*

Ask your group to turn to the article *The Gospel Helps Us Fight Fairly* in their Participant's Guide and read it aloud together, taking turns at the paragraph breaks.

DISCUSSION *10 minutes*

> **ASK**   Okay, let's see where we land on the spectrum . . . Who is an attacker? Who is a withdrawer?

> **ASK**   What things on the two lists in the article did you most identify with? (That is, how do you specifically tend to attack or withdraw?)

> **ASK**   Why do you think we handle conflict this way?

> **TRANSITION TO EXERCISE**   I think this exercise will help us not only discover why we attack and withdraw, but also how to move toward a gospel-centered approach to conflict.

EXERCISE *30 minutes*

Turn to the Gospel-Centered Conflict Resolution exercise and read through the chart together with your group.

> **ASK**   if there are any questions about the chart. Then give everyone time to complete the questions on their own.

> **SHARING**   After people have completed the questions, ask individuals in the group to talk about their responses. As people share about their situations and the ways they have wrongly dealt with them, invite the

group to help apply the gospel to those situations. In other words, what will gospel-driven conflict look like in that particular situation, in contrast to attacking or withdrawing?

WRAP-UP 5 minutes

Questions, comments, prayer.

lesson

9

ARTICLE

THE GOSPEL HELPS US FIGHT FAIRLY

How do you handle conflict? Do you attack? Or would you rather run? Are either of these ways of dealing with conflict "fighting fair"? Nothing is more common to relationships than conflict, but our ways of dealing with it are so instinctive that often we don't even think about how our faith should affect the way we handle it. If the gospel is not affecting the way we deal with conflict, then it's probably not touching us very deeply! This week we will consider how the gospel helps us fight fairly.

Think of the most recent argument or fight you've had. Maybe it was with your parents, a friend, a family member, or a classmate. Now set aside the circumstances of the argument (what the issue was, how it made you feel, who was right or wrong, etc.) and take a moment to consider your actions during the conflict. Your behavior probably falls into one of two categories.

Some people are **attackers**. They like to be on the offensive. They place a high value on justice so it matters greatly to them who is right and who is wrong. The following are signs that you might be an attacker:

- You deal with anger or frustration by "venting" it.
- You argue your case passionately.
- You ask questions like "How do you know?" and "Can you prove that?"
- You cross-examine like a lawyer in order to get to the bottom of things.
- Winning the argument is often more important than loving the person.

On the other end of the spectrum are **withdrawers**. People with this tendency often find themselves on the defensive. They tend to avoid or ignore conflict and, when pressed into an argument, they are usually silent or passive. If you're a withdrawer, here are some patterns you might recognize:

- You deal with anger or frustration by suppressing it.
- You have opinions but keep them to yourself in order to "keep the peace."
- You ask questions like, "Do we have to talk about this now?" And, "Does it really matter?"
- You'd rather avoid a fight than win one.
- You sometimes physically leave an argument in order to "get some space."

These are typical ways we respond to disagreement, frustration, offense, or hurt. The fact that these responses are considered "normal" (i.e., natural) is a clue that they may not be biblical (i.e., supernatural).

How, then, do we move toward resolving conflict in a biblical manner?

Gospel-centered confrontation mirrors God's movement toward us in the gospel. God did not pour out his wrath on us (attack) or remove his presence from us (withdraw). Instead, he sacrificially moved toward us in the person of Jesus, full of grace and truth. Jesus confronted sin, invited relationship, and provided a way of reconciliation. Thus, the gospel provides the pattern of biblical conflict resolution. We have a proper motivation (love), confidence (faith), and means for resolving conflict (grace and truth).

Motivation: To love someone is to be motivated by love so that we move toward them for their good. In other words, we don't seek resolution just because we want to feel better about things. So let's say your brother or sister wrongs you. You could bring it up because you want them to feel really bad (attacking), or you could not bring it up at all because that's just how they are (withdrawing). But love won't let you do either of these

Lesson 9 95

things. Love compels you to bring it up because you want them to experience the gospel by having a chance to repent of their sin and receive forgiveness. Love seeks the good of others, even when they sin against us.

Confidence: Resolving conflict is scary because there is always a chance that bringing it up will make things even messier: they could reject us again; they could say more hurtful things; we may never see things the same way and end up even more frustrated than before. Moving toward people, especially those who have hurt us, is risky and makes us vulnerable. That is why our confidence is not in ourselves or in them, but in Christ. We can pray and ask for God's help because we know that he desires people to be reconciled (Matthew 5:23-24). Further, we can risk rejection and hurt because we have acceptance and comfort in Christ. Of course those things will be hard, but they do not define us (2 Corinthians 3:4). Finally, even when things do not resolve, we can rest in the fact that God will make all things right (Romans 12:17-21).

Means: Sometimes the difficulty with resolving conflict is simply that we don't know what to do. It's like we want to fix our car, but we don't have the right tools. The gospel gives us the right tools to deal with conflict: grace and truth. After all, this is how Jesus reconciled us to God. He was full of grace and truth (John 1:14). God's grace means that we can come before him without fear of being condemned (Romans 8:1). Even though we have sinned against God, when we are in his presence we receive grace upon grace (John 1:16).

Many times, people attack and withdraw because they feel like they are being condemned. We can put them at ease by extending grace, which can take many forms: serving them, telling them up front we love them and want what is good for them, not talking badly about them to others, talking to them in private, admitting the ways we contributed to the conflict before talking about what they did, and so on. Grace means we try to see people as God sees all of us, as sinners in need of forgiveness.

Grace and truth go together. Grace seeks relationship; truth defines relationship. Conflict is evidence that things are not the way they are supposed to be. God made us for relationships, and we all have a basic sense of what constitutes a good friendship. We all value honesty, support, acceptance, understanding, and common interests. God hard-wired us with a desire for relationships and gave us all an innate sense of what they ought to be like.

Even more, he has put it in writing! The Bible is full of wisdom and instruction about how to love each other. Truth gives us a common goal in our conflict. Instead of trying to win each other over to what we want the relationship to be like, we can both look to God and his Word and pursue life with God together. This means that both parties will have to be honest about what God wants (what they should have done in the specific situation at hand), how they have fallen short of that (confess sin), and what it will take to restore the relationship.

The gospel calls us to repent of our sinful patterns of attacking and withdrawing. And the gospel empowers us to move into conflict by faith, with a humble, confident, God-glorifying intentionality. We can forsake the "normal" way of doing things for the gospel way.

lesson

9

EXERCISE

GOSPEL-CENTERED CONFLICT RESOLUTION

How do you usually deal with conflict; do you tend toward attacking or withdrawing? Which descriptions above do you particularly identify with?

A GOSPEL-CENTERED APPROACH TO CONFLICT

Outlined below is a process of dealing with conflict in a gospel-centered manner. Each aspect is listed, along with some questions that will help you assess your tendencies in that area. You may call to mind past experiences or even a current conflict with someone. Remember, the goal is to recognize unhealthy patterns in your life and to practice applying the gospel more effectively.

1. WHAT DID I DO? In any conflict, everyone has something to "own." Identify your words and actions in the conflict. Were you defensive? Did you blame others? Were you really argumentative? Did you say mean things? Did you gossip to others about the person you are in conflict with? Did you lie? Did you not say what you should have because you were afraid of how they would respond? Did you avoid the person, hoping the problem would just disappear? Confess these things as sin to God and to those involved.

2. WHY DID I DO IT? What was the motive behind your words and actions: saving face, being right, revenge, insecurity, fear, etc.? By faith, affirm your trust in the power of the Holy Spirit to free you from these sins of pride and fear.

3. WHAT DO I DO NOW? Tell the other person that you want to talk about things and try to resolve the conflict. Talk honestly and respectfully about your thoughts and feelings, and invite the other person to do the same. Do you understand each other? What usually gets in the way of your understanding, or being understood (anger, argumentativeness, dishonesty, timidity, assumptions you make about others, etc.)? Specify what steps need to be taken toward resolution. Pray for God's will to be done (his glory and each other's good). Thank him for paying the ultimate price of death to resolve the ultimate conflict of our sinful rebellion against him.

NOTES

NOTES

NOTES

NOTES

mission
grace through you

At Serge we believe that mission begins through the gospel of Jesus Christ bringing God's grace into the lives of believers. It also sustains us and empowers us to go into different cultures bringing the good news of forgiveness of sins and new life to those whom God is calling to himself.

As a cross-denominational, reformed, sending agency with 200 missionaries on over 25 teams in 5 continents, we are always looking for people who are ready to take the next step in sharing Christ, through:

- **Short-term Teams:** One to two-week trips oriented around serving overseas ministries while equipping the local church for mission
- **Internships:** Eight-week to nine-month opportunities to learn about missions through serving with our overseas ministry teams
- **Apprenticeships:** Intensive 12–24 month training and ministry opportunities for those discerning their call to cross-cultural ministry
- **Career:** One- to five-year appointments designed to nurture you for a lifetime of ministry

   Grace at the Fray   Visit us online at: www.serge.org/mission

www.newgrowthpress.com

spiritual renewal
grace through you

Disciples who are motivated and empowered by grace to reach out to a broken world are handmade, not mass-produced. Serge intentionally grows disciples through curriculum, discipleship experiences, and training programs.

Curriculum for Every Stage of Growth

Serge offers grace-based, gospel-centered studies for every stage of the Christian journey. Every level of our materials focuses on essential aspects of how the Spirit transforms and motivates us through the gospel of Jesus Christ.

- 101: The Gospel-Centered Series
  (The Gospel-Centered Life, The Gospel-Centered Community)
- 201: The Gospel Transformation Series
  (Gospel Identity, Gospel Growth, Gospel Love)
- 301: The Sonship Course and Serge Individual Mentoring

Gospel Renewal for You

For over 25 years Serge has been discipling ministry leaders around the world through our Sonship course to help them experience the freedom and joy of having the gospel transform every part of their lives. A personal discipler will help you apply what you are learning to the daily struggles and situations you face, as well as, modeling what a gospel-centered faith looks and feels like.

Training to Help You Disciple Better

Serge's discipler training programs have been refined through our work with thousands of people worldwide to help you gain the biblical understanding and practical wisdom you need to disciple others so they experience substantive, lasting growth in their lives. Available for onsite training or via distance learning, our training programs are ideal for ministry leaders, small group leaders or those seeking to grow in their ability to disciple effectively.

 Grace at the Fray   Visit us online at www.serge.org/mentoring

www.newgrowthpress.com

curriculum for every stage of growth
grace through you

Every day around the world, Serge teams help people develop and deepen the living, breathing, growing relationship with Jesus that the gospel promises. We help people connect with God in ways that are genuinely grace-motivated and that increase their desire and ability to reach out to others. No matter where you are along the way, we have a series that is right for you.

101: The *Gospel-Centered* Series

Our *Gospel-Centered* series is simple, deep, and transformative. Each *Gospel-Centered* lesson features an easy-to-read article and provides challenging discussion questions and application questions. Best of all, no outside preparation on the part of the participants is needed! They are perfect for small groups, those who are seeking to develop "gospel DNA" in their organizations and leaders, and contexts where people are still wrestling with what it means to follow Jesus.

201: The *Gospel Transformation* Series

Our *Gospel Transformation* studies take the themes introduced in our 101 level materials and expand and deepen them. Designed for those seeking to grow through directly studying Scripture and working through rich exercises and discussion questions, each *Gospel Transformation* lesson helps participants grow in the way they understand and experience God's grace. Ideal for small groups, individuals who are ready for more, and one-on-one mentoring, *Gospel Identity*, *Gospel Growth*, and *Gospel Love* provide substantive material, in easy-to-use, manageable sized studies.

The *Sonship* Course and Individual Mentoring from Serge

Developed for use with our own missionaries and used for over 25 years with thousands of Christian leaders in every corner of the world, Sonship sets the standard for whole-person, life transformation through the gospel. Designed to be used with a mentor, or in groups ready for a high investment with each other and deep transformation, each lesson focuses on the type of "inductive heart study" that brings about change from the inside out.

 Grace at the Fray   Visit us online at www.serge.org/resources

www.newgrowthpress.com